THE POLITICS OF

RELIGIOUS
CONFLICT

RICHARD E. MORGAN, assistant professor
of public law and government at Columbia
University, is a consultant to the Center for
Research and Education in American Liberties at Columbia. The editor of a new series
of books on American politics for Pegasus,
he is a graduate of Bowdoin College and
received a doctorate in government from
Columbia University. He will be a fellow in
law and government at the Harvard Law
School during the academic year 1968-69.

ABOUT THE AUTHOR

Richard E. Morgan, assistant professor of public law and government at Columbia University, is a consultant to the Center for Research and Education in American Liberties at Columbia. The editor of a new series of books on American politics for Pegasus, he is a graduate of Bowdoin College and received a doctorate in government from Columbia University. He will be a fellow in law and government at the Harvard Law School during the academic year 1968–1969.

THE POLITICS OF
RELIGIOUS
CONFLICT

Church and State in America

by RICHARD E. MORGAN

PEGASUS  NEW YORK

THE POLITICS OF RELIGIOUS CONFLICT
is part of a series, "Studies in Contemporary
American Politics," published by Pegasus under
the General Editorship of Richard E. Morgan,
Columbia University.

FOR MY PARENTS

PREFACE

I have written this book on a very simple plan. First, I utilize certain conceptual equipment of contemporary political science to analyze a particularly confusing sort of civic conflict which can be called the politics of church and state. My intent is to dissect this "politics" for examination and, hopefully, to increase our understanding of it. Second, I attempt, on the basis of this analysis, to suggest what may happen to the politics of church and state in the 1970's and 1980's— to weigh the potential for future civic conflict inherent in church-state issues.

I have accumulated many debts in the course of my work on church-state matters. To the Survey Research Center of the University of California at Berkeley, I am indebted for the data on Protestant attitudes toward Catholics which appear in Chapter I. The American Jewish Congress kindly gave permission for the reproduction of its *Litigation Docket*. Table 1 and Figure 1 are reproduced by permission of the *American Political Science Review* and the authors.

It would make a very long list if I were to try to mention every individual who has given up time to help me. Let me rather thank them all, and ask forgiveness of those who will disagree or be offended by what I say. My colleagues George La Noue and James Connor read portions of the manuscript and saved me from many errors. Marc Rohr and Lynda Connor helped me greatly with the mechanics of the final draft.

It is customary in a first book to mention one's teachers, but in this case much more is involved than convention. My first teacher, Athern P. Daggett, of Bowdoin, must bear considerable responsibility for my launching into political science. He has contributed hours of good talk over the years and read many parts of early drafts. David B. Truman, of Columbia, first focused my attention on the intellectual advantages of analyzing politics in terms of interest group interaction, and vulgarizations of his ideas occur frequently in my writing. Finally, Alan F. Westin, of Columbia, as teacher, colleague, and friend, has contributed in innumerable ways to my study of church-state relations. All the above, of course, must be absolved of specific responsibility for what follows.

To my wife Eva Corliss Morgan, who has spent many frustrating hours over the typewriter in aid of these pages, I owe any stylistic graces which have slipped into the text.

Richard E. Morgan
Columbia College
Whitsuntide, 1968

CONTENTS

INTRODUCTION

There can be little question that the United States has entered into a period of unusually rapid social change. Some of this change, it is hoped, will be purposeful and governmentally managed. Yet especially in the areas of education and social welfare, multiplying objective needs are outstripping the capacity of politicians (using that word in its broadest sense) to bargain, accommodate and build coalitions of support for governmental innovations. One problem which afflicts politicians working in the areas of education and social welfare is conflict over the proper relationship between the government and the churches. I propose to analyze church-state conflict in terms of the organized groups which are the principal combatants.

In a sprawling and diverse political system such as ours, any significant innovation in domestic policy will disturb the existing pattern of group interests and make its authors a focus of controversy. Some groups will see themselves as benefiting by a new pattern, others will feel themselves deprived and disadvantaged. It is the craft of the politician to steer a course through such choppy waters, tacking and trimming, and finally implementing that for which he has managed to marshal some consensus and which he has been able to protect from predators. The literature of American politics is rich in studies of the interest-group interaction around such problems as taxation, conservation, agriculture and the regulation of business. Political scientists and politically concerned citizens have available to them excellent studies of business groups, labor groups and organizations representing ethnic interests. It is generally recognized that if one wishes to understand a particular conflict a very useful way of going about it is to identify and investigate the organized groups making claims and counterclaims on each other and on society as a whole. Group motivation (the nature of group interests) can be assessed; the composition and relative cohesiveness of constituencies can be considered and perhaps measured; the resources for political warfare—talent, money, followers, and prestige to name a few—can be catalogued and compared; and the relationships between groups can be detailed.

Of course such interest-group analysis will not provide a *sufficient* understanding of our political life, or even of the politics of a single conflict area. One also needs to study the governmental institutions involved, the moral and philosophical aspects of choices to be made, the historical development of the problem, and factors in the larger political environment (foreign policy considerations, for instance) which influence the conflict with which one is concerned. But some comprehension of the play of interest group forces is *necessary* to achieve intellectual control over any particular conflict.

Today, church-state problems constitute only a small part of the political difficulties which beset educational and social welfare innovators, and though considerable heat has been produced by the church-state clashes which have marked the 1960's, these conflicts are less important and difficult than conflicts over race relations, hardcore poverty and urban blight (although these letters are often complicated by church-state issues). Recognizing this, it is still strange that American political science has produced so little analysis of the politics of church and state. Church-state conflict promises to give our leaders trouble for some time to come, and it will be useful to know something about who the claimants are, what they feel is at stake and how they operate.

One clarification must be made at the outset. The clashing groups and the contradictory claims which swirl around the problem of the relationship of religion to the public order have given rise to a number of fascinating constitutional and philosophical questions. These are treated by David R. Manwaring in his companion volume to this study, *Religion, Liberty, and the State,* and it is not part of my task to explore them in detail. I will touch on them, but only to describe the positions of the combatants. Manwaring is concerned with how the judiciary, and especially the Supreme Court, develops legal principles in an attempt to adjust contemporary church-state problems; I am concerned with why there *are* problems, and with the political dynamics of church-state conflicts.

Organizationally, it seemed best to begin with the causes of conflict over church-state relations. I offer a tentative classification in Chapter I in terms of "underlying tension," "trigger issues" and "emerging issues." In Chapter II, the principal church-state interest groups are surveyed, and an attempt is made to suggest the patterns of conflict and cooperation among them. With this treatment of tensions and groups as background, Chapter III identifies three "arenas" of church-state conflict, and includes brief case studies of the style of politics in each arena. Chapter IV (a longer case study) traces the development of a bitter church-state battle which raged in New York during 1966 and 1967. This is intended to illustrate the interrelations of the arenas of conflict and to reflect the divisive quality of church-state issues. The concluding chapter is a very brief essay in what is becoming modishly known as "futureology."

THE POLITICS OF

RELIGIOUS
CONFLICT

CHAPTER ONE

SOURCES OF
CHURCH-STATE CONFLICT

The reasons *why* groups struggle—the tensions which animate the "issues"—must not be lost sight of in the haste to discuss the tactics of group action. Without some understanding of group motivations much about any political conflict will remain opaque. A group's persistence in an extreme position or its refusal to cooperate with seemingly attractive allies may involve basic motivating forces. If one wishes to understand why a conflict arises, persists or dies, it is not enough to ask what groups do. It is also necessary to explore the fears and needs which shape group goals.

In the politics of church and state, one can identify important sources of tension that underlie and are relatively remote from the daily *sturm und drang;* one can sort out immediate issues which trigger today's political conflicts; and one can spot certain emerging issues which seem likely to complicate things increasingly as time goes by.

UNDERLYING SOURCES OF TENSION

At the most basic level it must be noted that differences of religious ideology produce very different "civic" attitudes concerning the proper relationship between religious institutions and public authority. Despite the difficulty of generalizing about such matters, it is clear that Catholics operate from different premises concerning church-state relations than do Baptists; Jews and non-believers differ from both of these and from each other. It is with these varying conceptions of the nature of man, the state and the religious enterprise that discussion of

church-state tensions must begin. From this, we can move on to consider two further underlying sources of tension: animosity between
creeds and differences in church structures.

Ideology

It is a cliché—and that is a mark of its truth—that until well into
the present century, America was a "Protestant nation." Not that all
or even most of the people were regular churchgoers, but in a cultural
sense Protestant ideas and Protestant spokesmen commanded the
heights of our society. Protestant notions of individualism, equality
and congregational democracy interlocked with and supported the prevailing political ideologies of face-to-face government and laissez faire.
Authority and centralization in religion were held to be incompatible
with democracy, and political liberty went hand in hand with individual revelation through the scriptures. This culturally ascendant Protestantism did not require that one practice religion, but it did, and in a
modified form still does, require that those who aspire to public office
make stylized professions of belief.

There were exceptions, of course. Episcopalians have always found
it difficult to be democratic and anti-episcopal (although low church
enthusiasts have given it a mighty try), and as early as the 1870's
Protestant hegemony was being challenged in large cities. But large
cities were un-American anyway; and the Episcopalians were suspect
because of their Anglican association—which was both foreign and
establishmentarian. While the country was predominantly provincial,
it was predominantly "freechurch" Protestant.

Thomas Sanders, in his *Protestant Concepts of Church and State*,[1]
has described the welter of Protestant ideas concerning religion and
the public order, and suggested the difficulty of speaking of a single
Protestant position. Nevertheless, there are several important doctrinal
themes which run through most Protestant thinking on the subject. It
is not too much to say that for major elements within the Protestant
community, historically and today, strict separation between the
churches and government is a doctrinal imperative—an important element of the religious ideology. The reasons for this have to do with the
diverse and fragmented nature of American Protestantism, and with its
negative conception of the state.

No one should suppose that because so many different Protestant
bodies took root in America, they were tolerant of each other. Indeed,
the evidence from the colonial and revolutionary periods suggests the

reverse. Protestant bodies behaved in what the German historian of religion, Ernst Troeltsch, has described as typically "sectarian" fashion.[2] There was little real tolerance; much of the "religious freedom" which is supposed to have characterized early America resulted from the openness and sparsely settled nature of the country. Unorthodox belief or behavior was not tolerated, but the nonconformist could always turn his deviance into orthodoxy by walking out into the woods and setting up on his own.[3]

Only slowly, with increasing density of population, did an acceptance of diversity develop within proud and suspicious Protestant bodies no longer felt superior to one another. At first the "principle" lations which most people desired for psychological and economic reasons, to war against heretics when there now were so many close at hand. What is fascinating, however, is the way in which the growing practical acceptance was swiftly rationalized in terms of existing Protestant notions of independence and individualism and elevated into a theological principle which was widely accepted within the Protestant community by the middle of the nineteenth century.

One historian of American Protestantism, Winthrop Hudson, has described this principle as "denominational."[4] Its evolution did not imply that all sectarian feelings had evaporated, or that Protestant bodies no longer felt superior to one another. At first, the "principle" simply entailed a recognition that other brands of Protestantism were legitimate, and entitled to the same liberty claimed for oneself. But gradually Protestantism began to take pride in itself as a many-faceted and ruggedly individualistic enterprise. The house had many denominational mansions and it came to be seen as a source of strength that independent-minded worshipers could strike out on their own.

Thus the diversity of the Protestant witness was held to be the outward manifestation of freedom and anti-authoritarianism in religion, and this, in turn, came to be seen as the essence of the freechurch tradition. Voluntarism and privatism were the great virtues which followed from the principle of denominationalism; it might be regrettable that everyone could not worship in accordance with Baptist forms or Methodist forms or Presbyterian forms, but it would be a great evil if anyone's independence were jeopardized or if the centrifugal forces within American Protestantism were in any way artificially inhibited. All this fit with basic Protestant doctrine concerning individual revelation, and with American social circumstances. Religion, as a doctrinal matter, came to be viewed as a strictly private affair.[5]

The implications of denominationalism, voluntarism and privatism for the relationship between church and state were clear. The government, which could defeat voluntarism with coercive power and overcome privatism with its patronage, was the natural enemy of the free-church system. The free and open marketplace in religion could only be preserved if the corrupting, coercive, blundering state were kept entirely out. No attempt at impartiality by the state in aiding religion could avoid the ultimately disastrous effect which a lapse from privatism into publicly sponsored religion would have upon the free churches. A church should be regarded as just another private association, arranged to suit the members. In the words of the most influential Protestant theoretician of church and state, Roger Williams, it

> is like unto a Body or College of Physicians in a City; like unto a Corporation, Society or Company of East-Indie or Turkie-Merchants, or any other Society or Company in London; which Companies may hold their Courts, keep their Records, hold disputations; and in matters concerning their Society, may dissent, divide, break into Schisms and Factions, sue and implead each other at the Law, yea, wholly break up and dissolve into pieces and nothing.[6]

This theological rejection of establishment—including multiple establishment in which all religious bodies are supported impartially—has been characterized by Sidney E. Mead as "the lively experiment." It was new on the world religious scene and represented a distinctive contribution of American Protestantism.

Strict separation is, of course, only one strand in the tangled weave of Protestant doctrine, and it varies in its prominence throughout the whole. Baptists are more conscious of separationist doctrine than are Episcopalians, and Congregationalists fall somewhere in the middle. Yet even today, when other doctrines of American Protestantism are eroding and many church members are embarrassed by the old theologies, the strict separation of church and state remains a powerful notion around which broad Protestant support can be mobilized.[7]

Distinct from the general Protestant persuasion is another separationist ideology which is best called secularist. If Protestants have wished to protect religion from the state, secularists have wished to protect the state from religion. If the leading Protestant ideologist was Roger Williams, his secularist counterpart was certainly Thomas Jefferson. It is often suggested in the heat of church-state debates that secularism is a recent and undesirable growth in America and reflects a mid-twentieth century moral decay. This is nonsense. Secularism is a proud and important tradition in American thought, and its provenance is impeccably revolutionary. The Constitution of the United States was profoundly affected by the secular learning of the Enlightenment, and its principal architects were deists and agnostics. Despite the cultural pre-eminence achieved by Protestantism during the nineteenth century, many of the most influential political innovators of the late eighteenth century were only nominally faithful.

What is important for us about secularism is the way in which it has interlocked with Protestantism on the subject of church and state. For both, religion is a private, voluntary, and individual matter, with which the state has no concern whatever. Jefferson and Williams could agree that "compulsion stinks in God's nostrils," and that the secular state stood in exactly the same relation to a religious association as it did to one whose purpose was literary discussion or the companionable consumption of madeira. For quite opposite reasons, both traditions commanded that government keep out.

Close examination, of course, reveals differing inflections in the command. Protestants expect the state to avoid all involvements with organized religion, but to be "friendly." For some, this even includes a nonsectarian religious element in public education.[8] The secularist expects the state to be indifferent to organized religion, and is especially concerned (as was Jefferson) that religion, with its supposed antirational implications, not pollute education.[9] Throughout most of our history, however, the pace of government activity and intervention has been slow, and this has tended to reinforce similarities between the two views rather than to accentuate the differences.

The beliefs of American Jewry concerning religion and the public order have been more directly grounded in experience than those of Protestants and secularists. For Jews, a desire for separation of church and state derives less from fundamental assumptions about the nature of God and the state, than from the brutal lessons of Jewish history.

As a matter of theology, Jews are not optimistic rationalists in the Enlightenment tradition; they do not view religious associations as the result of purely voluntary identification and activity. As Richard Rubenstein has pointed out, "there is nothing voluntary about the normative conception of membership in the Jewish community."[10] What makes separationists of American Jews is the conviction that in Christian countries where the state is a supporter of religious activity, Jews are apt to be made uncomfortable. The best chance of living decently in a community with a Christian majority is assured by a scrupulously secular state—a state which does not inculcate, support or interact in any way with religion. Thus a small religious minority, whose relations with the religious majority have been fraught with tension and trauma, seeks salvation in secularization. Any supportive relationship between religion and the public order appears likely to work to its disadvantage by increasing the importance of religion and, necessarily, the sense of religious differences. It is precisely this sense of difference which Jews wish to see minimized.

Thus we have another prescriptive harmony; Jews favor many of the same separationist outcomes as Protestants and secularists. Again, there are differing emphases within the Jewish community, and some vigorous dissent from the prevailing separationist persuasion on the part of Orthodox Jews. In general, however, the ideological predisposition continues strongly separationist.

Roman Catholic thought, of course, gives rise to policy prescriptions substantially at variance with those endorsed by the other three traditions. Here are contradictions which no amount of good will can exorcise as long as the parties continue to take their traditional ideologies seriously. No matter how carefully the problem is parsed, Catholics take a favorable view of cooperative relations between government and religious institutions.

The contradiction between the Catholic and Protestant positions is rooted in their differing views of the state. The Catholic legal theorist Norman St. John-Stevan has remarked that:

> The Catholic starts with the conception of the good but damaged natural man: the Protestant with an idea of man utterly corrupted by the Fall. For the Catholic the state would have been necessary for man had he remained a perfect being; for the Protestant it is the direct result of original sin. For Luther the world was an inn, and the devil its landlord. The employment of [state] power to further social and religious ends seems reasonable to Catholics, but Protestants, at least in theory, are distrustful of all worldly power, as contaminated by sin.[11]

This is a matter which goes deeper than canards about Catholic yearnings for the established and preferred position which the church has known throughout most of the Latin world. Few American Catholics dream such purple dreams. Many, however, are deeply offended by the notion that the state is not actively committed on the side of religion against atheism and indifference.

Contemporary American Catholic thought on the subject is perhaps best represented by the late John Courtney Murray, S.J., a theologian and philosopher who devoted much attention to church-state problems in the United States and the proper Catholic responses to them. In a collection of essays dealing with the general topic of religion and the public order, Murray rejected the phrase "separation of church and state," and referred rather to the *distinction* between church and state.[12] He argued that the "first article of the American political faith is that the political community, as a form of free and ordered human life, looks to the sovereignty of God as the first principle of its organization," and he favored cooperative arrangements between government and religious institutions on a carefully limited and nondiscriminatory basis.[13] Thus, whether one looks to sophisticated Catholic commentators such as Murray, Robert Drinan,[14] and Jerome Kerwin,[15] or to somewhat less subtle writers such as William O'Brien[16] and James M. O'Neill,[17] one finds deep skepticism about the wisdom and historical foundation of the relatively separationist line which the United States Supreme Court has taken during the last twenty years, and which culminated in 1963 in decisions banning compulsory prayer and Bible reading in the public schools. These latter cases are a cause of special pain.

This "accommodationist" predisposition (favoring cooperative arrangements between churches and the state) gives rise to a reading of the Constitution's religious clauses which differs radically from the Protestant reading. Catholics find it difficult to accept a theory of the First Amendment which holds religion to be a purely private concern toward which the state is morally neutral—a theory in which the state has no legitimate interest in the relationship of men to God. Yet precisely that assertion is at the heart of the Protestant separationist theory and is concurred in, albeit for different reasons, by secularists and Jews. Father Murray is quite prepared to accept a distinction between church and state on prudential grounds (as a "treaty of peace"). But if the First Amendment is held to mean that churches are, in regard to the state, simply "private associations organized for particular purposes" (a company of "Turkie-Merchants") then "there are immediately 35 million dissenters, the Catholic community."[18] The state, they believe, must recognize the special and transcendental mission of the religious institutions. It must be morally committed to their success. Mutually advantageous arrangements should be worked out in a pragmatic fashion, recognizing always the disparate natures and functions of church and state, and taking into account

the sensibilities of others as is necessary and right in a pluralistic society. Seen from the respective separationist viewpoints this is not
nearly good enough.

Certainly such abstract considerations are not the only source of
church-state conflict. We are not dealing with glassy-eyed ideologues
assaulting one another because their theologies demand it. Ideological
contradictions are, however, part of the context of controversy. Without
an appreciation of them, our understanding of the politics of church
and state will lack an important dimension.

Psychology

Related but intellectually distinct from ideological differences are
creedal antipathies. We must leave it to psychologists to develop a pre-
cise definition of "prejudice," and determine the extent to which it is
bred by ideological contradictions. For us it is enough that there are
unreasoning fears and emotional antagonisms which, no matter what
their origins, contribute to church-state conflicts. These emotional antipathies are more difficult to pinpoint and discuss than ideological differences, and an attempt to describe, for instance, Catholic anti-semitism,
carries one into foul and penumbral regions. Yet no one can understand church-state problems without recognizing that currents of anti-
Catholicism still surge through parts of American Protestantism, and
that long experience as a minority faith (a poor and ethnically "inferior" minority at that) has left significant portions of the Catholic
community viscerally hostile to, and sullenly uncomprehending of, the
Protestant free-church tradition.[19]

None of the ideological traditions has a monopoly on emotional
hostility. There are at least six variants which are relevant to the
politics of church and state. Protestant anti-Catholicism is no longer
the rough nativism which Billington and Higham described,[20] but is
usually expressed as a conviction that the Catholic Church is infinitely
dangerous because it seeks to use worldly power—the literature
abounds in reference to the "wealth of Rome"—to turn the United
States into a "Catholic country." Secularist contempt for all religions,
but especially "dogmatic" Catholicism, appears in important sectors of
the liberal community. Jews often evince reflexive antipathy toward
the Catholic Church, remembering its history of anti-semitism and the
anti-semitism which continues to flourish in some countries where the
Church is dominant. Catholic suspicion of Protestants (as cultural imperialists) and Jews (as deicides) has already been mentioned; it only

remains to note the frequent uncivility of official Catholic statements concerning secularists—who are usually confused with the extreme continental anticlerics—in order to round out the picture.

Obviously, hostility levels are not constant, but vary considerably over time, perhaps disappearing completely. Anti-Catholic animus, for instance, seems to be cyclical, with outbreaks in the 1760's, 1830's, 1850's, 1870's, 1890's, 1920's and, I shall argue, late 1940's. The reasons for these surges are manifold, but in the case of the late 1940's a major element seems to have been "status anxiety." Daniel Bell and Richard Hofstadter have employed this concept to explain why certain elements of the population identified with Senator Joseph McCarthy's witch-hunts in the early 1950's,[21] and Joseph Gusfield used it in his analysis of the temperance movement within American Protestantism.[22] The suggestion is that when an aggregate of people— Protestants, new rich, small-town dwellers, or Catholics—experience dramatic alterations in their relative social positions anxiety results which heightens antipathies toward other social groupings. Thus a population losing status relative to its former social subordinates will tend to lash out with particular venom at newly ascendant elements, and the population enjoying an increase in status will try to consolidate its position and erase reminders of past inferiority. It seems unarguable that Protestants, and especially provincial Protestants, lost status rapidly in the years after 1930, while the formerly alien and proletarian Catholic community ascended into middle-class respectability. The transition from Protestant cultural and social dominance to a cultural triumvirate of "three great faiths" was not painless. It sharpened Protestant-Catholic antipathies and even evoked a specialized agency dedicated to containing hostilities—the National Conference of Christians and Jews.*

It might be objected at this point, however, that while all this is fine as literature it will not do as social science. Where is the data which demonstrates the existence of "antipathies"; and how, in any case, does one distinguish "emotional hostilities" from reasonable suspicions? After all, the Roman Catholic Church does countenance the persecution of Protestants in some parts of the world, and secularists may sincerely believe that it would be a better world if Catholicism would wither away. Are not the antipathies which one perceives simply a byproduct of conflict over substantive issues, rather than a source of

* The NCCJ was organized in response to the inter-religious strife of the 1928 presidential campaign.

tension? As for the suggestion that creedal antipathies are modulated by rising and falling status, the very notion of status anxiety (as used by Bell, Hofstadter and others) has been cogently criticized for imprecision and subjectivity.[23] What measures have we for judging the status movements of aggregates such as "Catholics"? Is it justifiable to think of "Catholics" and "Protestants" moving through status structure as aggregates rather than as individuals or small units such as extended families?

These are legitimate objections to which there can be no conclusive answers. Hard data (meaning data derived from survey research or depth interviewing) are scarce, and it was conceded at the outset of this discussion that the causal relationship between antipathy and political conflict is obscure. Yet it would be foolish to refrain from saying something about the psychological sources of church-state conflict simply because it cannot be said as precisely as one would like. Intuitive analyses (such as the status-anxiety approach) must be "tried on," not put aside until the future when our instruments of measurement may have improved.

Furthermore, there are some fragments of evidence which can be admitted and which may help to anchor discussion in this rather slippery area.

1. Looking back on the years immediately following World War II, it seems clear that the bitter church-state conflicts which occurred at the time were the result rather than the cause of heightened Protestant-Catholic antipathies.* By 1946 a new confidence and assertiveness had developed within the Catholic community which profoundly disturbed many Protestants. If the election of John F. Kennedy to the presidency in 1960 represented the coming of age of the American Catholic community, the Second World War represented the next-to-last step in the process of maturation.[24] Laity and hierarchy alike, Catholics emerged from the War eager to exert influence on a culture which they perceived as their own, rather than the private preserve of the Protestant middle class. Catholic utterances, typified by the annual statements of the bishops of the Administrative Board of the National Catholic Welfare Conference, took on a tone which many Protestants considered profoundly aggressive. The 1946 statement, which contained what many Protestants saw as presumptuous prescriptions for the conduct of

*Certainly the relationship may work the other way. Indeed, it will be the argument of this book that *today* the frequency with which church-state issues arise is probably serving to keep creedal antipathies alive.

American foreign policy, was typical.[25] Indications of increasing Protestant unease in the face of what Methodist Bishop G. Bromley Oxnam
dubbed a Catholic "cultural offensive" began to appear in the spring
of 1947 when various Protestant groupings held their annual conventions.* On May 7, the Council of Bishops of the Methodist Church
(at the time the largest Protestant denomination), met in Riverside,
California, and "accused the Roman Catholic Church of political activities in this country and abroad, which the council said amounted to
bigotry and denial of religious liberty."[26] Roman Catholic leaders in
the United States, the Council's report concluded, condoned anti-
libertarian practices "at the very moment that protestations of belief
in democracy are made . . . and demands for the public support of
parochial education are advocated as a contribution to the morality essential to freedom."[27] At the opening session of the meeting of the
Southern Baptist Convention in St. Louis, the Reverend Louie D. Newton, President of the Convention, declared that Protestants were "confronted by the most determined and adroit campaign to alter the traditional American understanding of the proper relationship of church
and state.[28] "The Baptist witness in behalf of the principle of separation of church and state," Newton declared, "should not be weakened
upon any pretext whatever."[29] The chronology of conflict seems to
support the status-anxiety analysis: Catholics were behaving like par-
venus, Protestants were over-reacting, and the old flames of animosity
were fanned. When church-state issues arose they precipitated major
confrontations. The great battles of the period (over the Supreme
Court's decision in the Everson Case, over President Truman's aid to
education proposals, and over the proposal for American diplomatic
representation at the Vatican) came *after* the spring of 1947; indications of sharpening antipathies had appeared well before that time.

2. Although the election of 1960 may represent the beginning of a
secular decline in anti-Catholic animus, some voting patterns were revealed which are hard to explain on any other grounds than dislike and

*In an attempt to chart the level of tension between Protestants and Catho-
lics in the immediate postwar period, the Catholic sociologist John J. Kane
examined the magazines *The Christian Century* and *America,* counting the number of editorials, articles, or letters critical of Catholicism (in *The Christian
Century*) or Protestantism (in *America*) for the years 1939, 1944 and 1949.
Kane worked out, for his selected years, the ratios of critical articles to the total
number of articles (excluding the small number of letters) carried by each
periodical. His results suggested a rather dramatic amplification of hostility.
John J. Kane, *Catholic-Protestant Conflict in America* (Chicago: Regnery,
1955).

fear of Roman Catholicism. In the most rigorous investigation of the 1960 results, Philip E. Converse, Angus Campbell, Warren E. Miller and Donald E. Stokes, of the Survey Research Center of the University of Michigan, found rather surprising defections of regular Democratic "party-identifiers" who had voted for Stevenson in 1956 and then swung to Nixon. This tendency was most evident in the South (Table 1), and correlated strongly with high Protestant church attendance (Figure 1). The Campbell group's conservative estimate of John F. Kennedy's net loss on "the religious issue" was 2.2 percent of the total vote (roughly the difference between a 52–48 victory and a 50–50 tie). Now it is possible that all those Democrats who voted against Kennedy because of his religion did so out of the reasoned conviction that a Roman Catholic in the White House would be a dangerous thing. There is certainly a case which can be made for such a stance, and many distinguished Americans are persuaded by it. Yet it taxes the imagination (and flies in the face of all that political scientists have learned about voting behavior) to suppose that such reasoned deliberation was a major factor in the anti-Catholic vote of 1960. It seems much more likely that the bulk of the religious defection from the Democratic candidate resulted from ancient, unreasoning antipathy to the Church of Rome.

3. A final interesting bit of data comes from the Survey Research Center of the University of California at Berkeley. Under a grant from the Anti-Defamation League of B'nai B'rith, the Center has been conducting an intensive study of anti-semitism in America. One part of this study sought to discover the extent of anti-Semitic attitudes with nine Protestant denominations, and the interview schedule used to generate the data also included a number of questions concerning Protestant attitudes toward Catholics. Again, the answers given to the Berkeley questions do not necessarily reflect the sort of antipathy which I am endeavoring to describe. As with the anti-Catholic voting of 1960, it is possible for a person to respond negatively from reasoned conviction. Yet the directions shown in the data are suggestive. Substantial percentages within all the denominations thought it "tends to be true" that Catholics seek to impose their religion on others (Table 2). Significant percentages felt that the American Catholic community seeks to advance its own interests through bloc voting (Table 3). Deep suspicion of the Catholic Church abroad is reflected in Table 4. (Interestingly, the study also found considerable anti-semitism among both Catholic and Protestant respondents.)[30] In most

TABLE 1

OFFSETTING EFFECTS OF THE CATHOLIC ISSUE, 1960 DEMOCRATIC PESIDENTIAL VOTE

Area	% of 2-party vote in area
Outside the South, Kennedy's "unexpected" . . .	
Gains from Catholics	5.2%
Losses from Protestant Democrats and Independents	−3.6
NET	+1.6%
Inside the South, Kennedy's "unexpected" . . .	
Gains from Catholics	0.7%
Losses from Protestant Democrats and Independents	−17.2
NET	−16.5%
For the **nation as a whole,** Kennedy's "unexpected" . . .	
Gains from Catholics	4.3%
Losses from Protestant Democrats and Independents	−6.5
NET	−2.2%

Source: Campbell, Converse, Miller and Stokes, "Stability and Change in 1960," 55 *American Political Science Review* at 278

FIGURE 1

DEFECTIONS TO NIXON AMONG PROTESTANT DEMOCRATS AS A FUNCTION OF CHURCH ATTENDANCE.

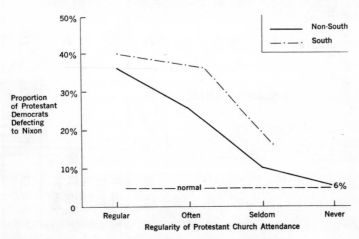

Source: Campbell, Converse, Miller and Stokes, "Stability and Change in 1960," 55 *American Political Science Review* at 277

TABLE 2

Reply to: Catholics try to impose their religious practices on others, answers are in % with "Don't knows" not shown. N = 3,000

	CONGREGATIONAL	METHODIST	EPISCOPAL	DISCIPLES OF CHRIST	PRESBYTERIAN	LUTHERAN (L.C.A. & A.L.C.)	AMERICAN BAPTIST	LUTHERAN (MO. SYNOD)	SOUTHERN BAPTIST
TRUE	11	16	19	14	23	18	18	23	25
TENDS TO BE TRUE	31	30	31	34	26	32	28	41	16
TENDS TO BE FALSE	31	31	23	28	23	23	26	16	38
FALSE	21	19	23	18	22	21	21	15	16

Source: Survey Research Center, University of California at Berkeley

TABLE 3

Reply to: Catholics tend to vote as a bloc for Catholic political candidates. Answers are in % with "don't knows" not shown. N=3,000

	CONGREGATIONAL	METHODIST	EPISCOPAL	DISCIPLES OF CHRIST	PRESBYTERIAN	LUTHERAN (L.C.A. & A.L.C.)	AMERICAN BAPTIST	LUTHERAN (MO. SYNOD)	SOUTHERN BAPTIST
TRUE	22	31	37	28	39	28	38	41	43
TENDS TO BE TRUE	45	44	35	36	36	38	36	27	39
TENDS TO BE FALSE	17	13	13	28	11	16	12	16	8
FALSE	9	7	10	2	7	10	6	7	4

Source: Survey Research Center, University of California at Berkeley

TABLE 4

Reply to: Protestants are not given religious freedom in Catholic countries the way Catholics are given freedom here. Answers in % with "Don't knows" not shown. N=3,000

	TRUE	TENDS TO BE TRUE	TENDS TO BE FALSE	FALSE
SOUTHERN BAPTIST	58	24	5	5
LUTHERAN (MO. SYNOD)	34	21	16	15
AMERICAN BAPTIST	37	35	10	5
LUTHERAN (L.C.A. & A.L.C.)	24	22	22	13
PRESBYTERIAN	42	24	13	9
DISCIPLES OF CHRIST	40	28	18	6
EPISCOPAL	28	25	20	16
METHODIST	29	31	20	7
CONGREGATIONAL	26	32	17	13

Source: Survey Research Center, University of California at Berkeley

cases the Southern Baptists, the Protestant denomination which can be intuitively identified as harboring intense emotional antipathy toward the Catholic Church, returned the highest negative response. Those denominations which can be intuitively identified as more urbane and tolerant of Catholicism—Episcopalians and Congregationalists—had lower negative scores.

The ecumenical spirit of the mid-1960's has certainly reduced the antipathies which flared in the late 1940's. Catholics now interact much more freely with Protestants; priests sit on the various committees of the American Civil Liberties Union and are regularly seen around the luncheon tables of the National Council of Churches. Fordham and other leading Catholic institutions have appointed Protestants to their theological faculties, and there is increasing experimentation with joint worship services and cooperative social-service ventures. But while all this is encouraging, it is well to remember that we are less than a decade away from the election of 1960, and the Berkeley research into Protestant attitudes was done in 1963.

Structure

Distinct from both ideological contradictions and creedal antipathies is the question of differing church interests. Here analysis is easier; we need not deal in doctrinal abstractions and nuances of emotion. We are on the firmament of budgets and buildings, and are concerned with how differences in the organization and operation of religious bodies (their respective *structures*) create differing vested interests—interests which will be differentially affected by changes in the status quo between church and state.

It is obvious that different churches do different things in different ways. Outside of unrestricted cash grants to be employed as the respective religious bodies see fit, it is difficult to see how governmental aid can ever be "neutral" or "equal" in its impact on as diverse a set of bodies as the American churches and synagogues. To take an easy but important example, the Roman Catholic Church places great stress upon educating the young. This is not an incidental social service, but a crucial aspect of its ministry. The massive apparatus of Catholic elementary and secondary education (serving almost 6 million students) is an important way in which the Church goes about its business of fishing for souls. The Southern Baptist Convention does not minister through elementary and secondary education, has not invested in it and sees it as an essentially secular function. It places great emphasis on revivals, Sunday schools and foreign missions as ways of realizing its ministerial goals.* If government gives aid to all church-related elementary and secondary schools, it may benefit these schools equally, but it benefits religious institutions differently. I do not advance this as an argument for denying public aid to sectarian schools; any of us in our armchairs may think that impartial aid to nonpublic schools is fair or unfair to churches. The fact is that Southern Baptists will not care for the idea, and the political analyst must take this into account.

By the same token, religious institutions which have invested in hospitals are likely to view aid to all nonpublic medical facilities differently from a group such as the Jehovah's Witnesses which relies on noninstitutional forms of ministry and is suspicious of medicine—especially medicine linked to what it regards as a hostile church. Religious bodies are still competitive and, to varying degrees jealous. A governmental decision which just happens to help one but not another can cause mighty outrage. Churches with little real property look quite differently on proposals to tax church-owned buildings than those whose holdings are large. The differences in structure and interest patterns are evident even in that hardy perennial of church-state politics, the debate over the propriety of military chaplains. From time to time, some hard-nosed separationist will argue that the federal government should not be paying for priests and preachers and chapels. To such arguments Father Edward Duff has given the following response:

> A Baptist boy can presumably open his Bible in the barracks, and inspired by the revelations it contains, satisfy his essential religious needs. Not so for the Catholic. Draft him for a part of his life where he is deprived of access to a priest, an instrument he believes irreplaceable to forgive his sins and to give him the Bread of Life, and you have egregiously, if thoughtlessly, trampled on his religious freedom. . . . Moreover, authoritative teaching is of [Catholicism's] essence.[31]

With Protestants, secularists, Jews and Catholics divided by ideologies, antipathies and structural disparities, the stage is set for conflict. This occurs when an issue arises which requires public officials to allocate community resources.

---

*The Southern Baptist Convention does support colleges and it is just at this point, where its structure is similar to that of Roman Catholicism, its strict separationism is beginning to wear thin.

TRIGGER ISSUES

Church-state encounters have become more frequent and sharp in recent years because rapid social changing is forcing specific questions concerning the relationship of religion to the public order. These trigger issues may be roughly classified under the rubrics *governmentalization of welfare services* and *educational revolution.*

The Governmentalization of Welfare

The accelerated development of the American welfare state has ominous implications for the church-state status quo. Each time a government—federal, state or local—moves into a new social service field, administrative structures must be created or existing private institutions subsidized. There is a great deal of governmental money now becoming available for welfare, and religious institutions are often in positions to take advantage of it. Many churches have highly developed welfare bureaucracies. They are operating hospitals, orphanages, food distribution centers, schools and homes for the aged. They can claim expertise and can offer to put the public dollar to work immediately with low overhead. A powerful argument is made that while there is great unfinished business in American society and overseas, government should enlist all possible allies in getting on with it. If religious institutions stand ready to help, why should they not be supported in these essentially secular pursuits?

Church-state questions have arisen at the federal level with regard to, among others, the "Hill-Burton" hospital program, the "PL 480" surplus food program, the surplus property disposal program, the Peace Corps, the War on Poverty (programs under the Economic Opportunity Act of 1964), and Medicare. Programs now contemplated by planners, such as a highly capitalized program for the care of the aged, will present the same sort of church-state issues.[32] Instances of local and state welfare funds being channeled through religious institutions are commonplace, with child care institutions leading the list. Many social service functions heretofore accomplished privately are being governmentalized. This is necessary, indeed inevitable, as the society becomes more complex and compacted. The costs of modern social services are becoming such that only government, with its taxing power, can bear them. But what is to be done with existing church-related structures? Are they to be integrated into the new publicly

financed welfare system, or are they to be left to wither away in private
with their functions pre-empted and their costs outstripping their capacity to pay?[33] This is a simplified and perhaps overdramatic statement of
the problem, but important choices are upon us. Statism is no longer a
bogie haunting the night of laissez faire, but rather the comfortable and
generally accepted American Way of Life. It is high time to ponder
the role of church-related institutions (and, indeed, all private
social-service institutions) in the national future. The alternatives have
not yet been clearly and publicly posed. But among the groups directly concerned with the problem, there is a growing sense that every
church-state engagement, fought over no matter how small a grant of
public funds, is part of a larger and, to them, vastly important struggle. As government spends more and does more, both the tension and
the perception of the stakes will increase. Ironically, the war in Viet
Nam is temporarily serving to contain the church-state conflict at
home. But as soon as increased federal funds become available for
welfare, the pace of church-state controversy can be expected to increase correspondingly.

The Educational Revolution

The American system of elementary and secondary education is presently undergoing rapid and far-reaching change. The reasons for this
are various, having to do with costs, technological change, new social-
scientific insights, international competition, the rise from quiescence
of the Negro community and the development of a secular and urban-
oriented mass culture. The implications of this "revolution" for the
politics of church and state can be suggested briefly.

We have noted that the Catholic community continues to view education as a vital part of their exercise of religion. The Church spends
hundreds of millions a year in this effort; it turns away more and more
children who cannot be accommodated; its existing educational plant
is overcrowded and distressingly obsolescent; as religious vocations are
declining and fewer nuns are available, it is forced to compete for lay
teachers on the open market. According to Catholic educators, there
simply is not enough money to keep up with the Catholic birth rates,
not enough money to expand, and not enough to furnish a 1970-style
education for those presently enrolled (see Table 5).[34]

As with welfare services, the costs of primary and secondary education are rising steeply. Many independent schools, especially the
Roman Catholic parochial schools which are based on the parish unit,

TABLE 5

ELEMENTARY AND SECONDARY SCHOOL PUPILS
IN THE UNITED STATES

Elementary Level (K-8)

Public Schools	31,200,000
Roman Catholic Schools	5,000,000
Other Non-public	400,000

Secondary Level (9-12)

Public Schools	12,000,000
Roman Catholic Schools	800,000
Other Non-public	500,000

Total Students
49,900,000

Source: latest available estimates from the U.S. Office of Education

are unwilling to raise tuitions and risk becoming exclusive prepschools. But with present sources of finance they declare themselves hard pressed to keep up with the salaries and facilities offered by the state schools. At the same time, for reasons not yet clearly understood but certainly having to do with the decay of our city centers and the traumas of racial desegregation, certain parts of the country are experiencing a middle-class movement away from the common schools. With more people desiring non-public (and often this means church-related) education for their children, there will come a demand for increased governmental support for independent schools. Defenders of the public school system, and there are many, deplore this trend, but it is increasingly suggested that the comprehensive common school system has outlived its usefulness—that America today requires a more pluralistic and diverse educational pattern.[35] John Courtney Murray posed the issue squarely:

One would expect that, as the pattern of society has altered and assumed a new pluralistic structure, so too would the patterns of the school system. The religious school would still remain "private" in a sense; it is a special kind of school which serves the religious and

educational needs of a particular community—the Catholic community, for instance. However, the change in the sociological status
of this particular community within the American community would
require some manner of corresponding change in the status of the
school system that it serves.[36]

Except for elite establishments, which can charge high tuition, no
group can hope to run competitive schools in the 1970's and 1980's
without substantial public support. Catholic schools constitute 90 percent of the church-related schools across the country. With each turn
of the economic screw the Catholic educator is forced closer to an
agonizing decision over where to cut back present programs. Some
Catholics advocate dispensing with the very expensive secondary
schools; others argue that adolescence is the critical period of intellectual and religious development, and that if something must go it should
be the early grades. With each new indication of Catholic interest in
governmental support, separationist concern rises over prospective di-
version of resources from the common schools to what they regard as
a sectarian and socially divisive purpose. The Berkeley findings on
Protestant attitudes toward Catholic schools are reflected in Table 6.

EMERGING ISSUES

It will have occurred to some by this point that I have not mentioned one frequently discussed type of church-state issue—governmentally sponsored religious exercises, especially prayer, Bible reading and holiday observance in public schools. Actually such issues
have only marginal political importance. They are volatile and capable
of generating a lot of emotion for a brief time, but they have little
long-range divisive potential because they do not involve allocation of
resources. It is the financial relationship of government to the churches
which the struggle is really about, and conflicts over religious ob-
servances are significant primarily because of their implications for
struggles over funds. These will be examined in Chapter III.

There are, however, two relatively unpublicized church-state issues
which deserve mention here. Neither is yet perceived as important, but
both are troublemakers. The first is the question of tax exemptions for
religious institutions; the second, the future of minority children, lower
class (as opposed to working class) children, and other such "unde-
sirables" if significant amounts of public money are given to church-
related and other independent schools.

TABLE 6

Reply to: By denying tax support to parochial schools, Protestants unfairly make Catholics support schools they do not use. Answers are in % with "Don't knows" not shown. N=3,000

	SOUTHERN BAPTIST	LUTHERAN (MO. SYNOD)	AMERICAN BAPTIST	LUTHERAN (L.C.A. & A.L.C.)	PRESBYTERIAN	DISCIPLES OF CHRIST	EPISCOPAL	METHODIST	CONGREGATIONAL
TRUE	8	5	6	7	5	6	9	7	7
TENDS TO BE TRUE	5	15	12	10	14	4	19	14	11
TENDS TO BE FALSE	15	14	18	20	19	22	19	21	24
FALSE	63	54	50	52	53	62	46	52	54

Source: Survey Research Center, University of California at Berkeley

God and Taxes

With more and more enterprises being undertaken by government at all levels, there is mounting concern among students and politicians over shrinking tax bases and tax "loopholes." Local governments, which bear much of the burden of housekeeping services such as schools, police and sanitation, must make do almost entirely with the real estate tax. States are adopting broad-based levies such as sales and income taxes. Increasing reliance is placed on the comprehensive taxing powers of the Federal Government, and Americans, until recently one of the most lightly taxed peoples on earth, are becoming highly conscious of the claims which the public sector now makes on their substance. In these circumstances, it is not surprising that traditional non-contributors to the general coffers receive careful scrutiny. It might have been all right to casually exempt religious institutions when government was doing little and when taxation did not hurt very many very much. But now that the pain has spread and increased, questions are being asked.

The practice of exempting socially preferred activities is, of course, built into our entire tax structure. Charitable and educational institutions of many sorts receive varying degrees of relief, but religious institutions are among the most favorably treated. Churches are benefited in three major ways: first, donations made to religious institutions are tax deductible; second, real property owned by churches is largely untaxed (in some states this includes both property used for worship *and* commercial property used for gain); third, income earned by churches on business activities and the rental of property is largely untaxed. Donations to educational institutions are also deductible, and real estate tax exemptions are granted on property used for educational purposes. But colleges and universities do pay income taxes on income from business activities.* Thus churches are measurably better off. It has been estimated that there is about $80 billion worth of untaxed church property in the United States and that the $700 million in New York City alone might produce $35 million per year in revenues.[37]

Today many churchmen and lay analysts are concluding that it is unconscionable for the substantial resources of organized religion in America to get off so lightly. On the "left" of this dispute are a number of strict separationists (predominantly Jews and secularists) who

---

*Neither religious nor educational institutions pay income tax on "passive" investments such as stocks and bonds.

contend that any exemption is unconstitutional. Worship, they argue, is a purely private affair and not a social service of the sort rendered by a university or a research foundation. To exempt such private activity is to place greater tax burdens on the community at large, thus flagrantly subsidizing religion. What is the difference in principle, they ask, between a direct grant and a tax exemption?

But the separationist camp is far from united on this matter. While some argue for no exemption at all, others hold that to allow taxation of places of worship and church incomes would place the churches at the mercy of the state and open the way for precisely the sort of governmental influence which the founding fathers sought to prevent. This is the position of many strict separationist Protestants, and, compounding irony and confusion, it overlaps with the approach of many accommodationists. Roman Catholic spokesmen, for instance, tend to echo John Marshall's dictum that the power to tax involves the power to destroy, and that while government should cooperate with and even support religion, the entire substance of the churches, including commercial activities which contribute to their sustenance and growth, should be immune. Taking a middle position are the bulk of separationists who feel that *some* exemption for the churches may be justifiable, but that some pruning back is necessary. Typically, these moderates would allow deductible contributions on the grounds that religion, while essentially private, has some social value as a humanizing and civilizing force. To ensure the free exercise of religion they would also continue exemption from real estate taxes of all property used for worship. Everything else, however, would be taxed at the usual rates; at the minimum, the churches should be brought in line with educational and other charitable institutions and pay taxes on business incomes. The normal separationist-accommodationist lines become blurred on the taxation issue, but this is no guarantee that conflict will not be generated when (as will happen with increasing frequency) attempts are made to change the status quo.

There has already been some activity on this front. During the late 1950's the Internal Revenue Service, urged on by vociferous separationist publicity, demanded back taxes from the Christian Brothers Winery in California. The Brothers paid $3.5 million in income tax under protest, and went to court claiming that their wine-making was a "sacerdotal" activity and that the tax violated the free-exercise clause. The courts upheld the IRS, but the precedent has not been vigorously employed against other church-related business.

The issue was brought into sharper focus in 1959 by one of the country's foremost churchmen, Eugene Carson Blake, a former stated clerk of the United Presbyterian Church and the President of the National Council of Churches, who announced that he favored greater taxation of the churches:

> One hundred years from now, the present pattern of religious tax exemption . . . , if continued, may present the state with problems of such magnitude that their only solution will be revolutionary expropriation of church property.[38]

And these sentiments were echoed by the *enfant terrible* of Episcopalians, James Pike, retired Bishop of San Francisco. In an article in *Playboy* magazine (a characteristically Pikeian jape at clerical convention), he asserted that "worldly power has seduced the church from its spiritual concerns of the past."[39] Separationist groups are becoming more concerned with tax issues. Americans United (Protestant) has been for years decrying the "hidden wealth" of the Roman Catholic Church; the American Jewish Congress has begun to make payments to New York City in lieu of taxes on its East Side headquarters, the Stephen Wise Congress House, and is urging this practice on all churches and synagogues; the American Civil Liberties Union has joined the battle, questioning continued exemption of unrelated business income.

Most significantly, however, the issue has already been the subject of one major court test. In 1963, Mrs. Madalyn Murray O'Hair, a litigious past president of the Free-Thought Society of America, brought suit in Maryland to end all exemption of real estate belonging to religious institutions. This effort was substantially aided by the American Jewish Congress, but the Maryland Court of Appeals (the highest in the state) upheld the exemptions as constitutional, and the United States Supreme Court refused to hear the case. There are other cases in progress raising the exemption question in other forms.

Structural differences between churches also complicate matters in this area. The largest potential "loser" in any alteration of the tax rules would be the Catholic Church. For reasons having to do with its proletarian character and costly ministerial style (schools, hospitals, convents) the Church in America has relied on entrepreneurship to a greater extent than any other religious body. It is extremely protective of its commercial activities, and can be counted on to fight back with all its impressive political power when these are threatened.

The Civil Rights Dimension

No other domestic political conflicts approach the intensity of those generated by the struggle of Negro Americans for entrance into the mainstream of community life. Civil rights politics (in the broad sense which includes Negro social and economic aspirations) is "tough," and special danger is thus presented when the politics of church-state and the politics of civil rights intersect. This is now happening on the question of state suport for church-related schools.

We have noted the way in which the middle-class drift away from public schools can be expected to increase the pressure behind demands for aid to non-public schools. If we are going to have more private schools it will be more difficult for strict separationists to hold the line. But the separationists, in turn, are finding new allies in the civil rights groups. Another dimension of interest and pressure is being added to an already bitter politics.

Separationists have been quick to point out the implications for racial integration of aid to non-public schools. The Reverend Dean Kelley of the National Council of Churches has put the matter plainly:

> Subsidizing private schools might *or might not* increase "equality" in elementary and secondary education in our nation, . . . [but] religious schools giving preference to their own members might succeed in carrying out a *de facto* form of racial segregation with federal funds . . .[40] (Emphasis in original.)

Kelley and other separationists are well aware that federal grants would carry with them the anti-discrimination provisions of the Civil Rights Act of 1964—no exclusion on racial grounds. Their point is that religious discrimination is not barred by the 1964 Act (the word religious in the prohibitive clause of the Act was removed at the specific behest of the National Catholic Welfare Conference), and the consequence of religious homogeneity is often a racial and class homogeneity which acts like a magnet for the white middle classes.

During 1965 and 1966 Catholic educators became aware of criticism from within the civil rights movement which asserted that parochial schools were becoming white havens. In October, 1966, the National Catholic Welfare Conference announced that its education department planned a racial census of Catholic schools to determine whether they were doing their part in aiding Negroes, but added defensively that only 2 percent of the nation's Negroes were Catholics, and that the predominantly white enrollment in the parochial schools simply reflected this fact.[41] Two months later Catholic discomfort concerning the social posture of their schools was increased by the findings of a distinguished Catholic educator, the Reverend Neil G. McCluskey, that parochial high schools were becoming increasingly elitist, and accepting chiefly well-prepared middle-class students.[42]

Early in 1967 the rumblings of civil rights activists began to be reflected in official policy. In February, the New York State Conference of the NAACP announced plans to raise an $800,000 war chest to oppose, among other things, any state aid to church-related schools. Dr. Eugene T. Reed, president of the Conference, stated that: "We are against aid in any way, shape or form, because it only helps those who would skirt legislation on desegregation."[43] As if in reply, the National Catholic Educational Association, meeting in Atlantic City, was urged by Msgr. James C. Donohue, educational director of the Catholic Conference, to make greater efforts toward integration, and a plan was launched for a national conference of parochial school administrators to consider the problem.[44] The next month, however, the civil rights issue arose in an even more vexing form in New Jersey where Democratic Governor Richard Hughes was shepherding through the legislature a bill requiring local authorities to furnish transportation subsidies to children attending non-public schools if this was being done for public school pupils (an existing statute only permitted such support at the option of the community). The state NAACP opposed the plan on the grounds that it would help whites to pull out of integrated schools. Separationists repeated these charges and added their usual church-state arguments.[45] The bill ultimately passed, but the significance of "civil rights separationism" was not lost on church-state professionals, and events in New York during this same time further cemented the alliance of the Negro leaders and strict separationists.

There is yet another complication to the "civil rights dimension" of the politics of church and state. At the very time that much of the civil rights movement is becoming separationist and anti-private-school, a small element within it is moving to support private schools for ghetto children.[46] This notion has been propounded by Christopher Jencks in the pages of *The Saturday Evening Post* and *The Public Interest;* and a great deal of thought is being devoted to it at the Lincoln Filene Center for Citizenship and Public Affairs of Tufts University.[47] The heart of this argument is that the public schools cannot do the job in the ghettos. The problem is not money (as usually supposed), but organization. The public schools, as governmental bureaucracies, more or less responsible to elected officials and necessarily governed by the elaborate rules which condition public spending and hiring, cannot achieve the flexibility necessary to cope with the culture of poverty. In a report prepared at the Lincoln Filene Center, Harvey Pressman has argued that:

> New, independent schools for the poor can provide a setting which is immediately receptive to the development, trial, and demonstration of the kind of experiment and innovation desperately needed in urban education and, indeed, in the whole education "industry." They can demonstrate, with high visibility and on a significant scale, that the children of the poor can learn as well as anybody else, when properly taught by people who believe in them. They can provide the "old" schools with some healthy competition.[48]

In answer to the objection of more traditionally-oriented civil rights leaders that such a course would result in less racial integration than the public school alternative, the proponents of the "ghetto-prep schools" suggest that white parents might be attracted by the excellence of these establishments, and that excellence is of far greater importance than the arithmetic of integration.

The difficulty, of course, is that while these new schools would be privately run, a large part of the costs would have to be borne by government. Any proposal to give any money to any non-public-school immediately raises the question, "what about the parochials?" As a practical political matter, it is difficult to envision aid going to any sort of non-public school without substantial aid going to church-related schools—especially church-related schools in decayed center-city settings. Separationist groups regard the proposals for ghetto private schools as a threat, and have denounced them as a sellout of the goal of racial integration in the common schools. Accommodationists increasingly are taking the line that the true interest of the Negro, and of all the deprived, is best served by the greatest possible aid to *all* schools, and that those who oppose such support reveal themselves as the "real" enemies of civil rights.[49]

CHAPTER TWO

THE DRAMATIS PERSONAE

The next step in achieving intellectual control over the politics of church and state is to identify the actual participants. Obviously aggregates such as Protestants and Catholics do not take political action. This is done by the specialized elites of organized groups which draw their support from differing sectors of the population. Who are these elites in the church-state struggle? What are their respective resources, strategies and biases? We have noted as a rule of political analysis that one does not understand a political struggle if one does not know the groups involved. Interest groups respond to the trigger issues and focus underlying tensions as they frame demands and bring them to bear on the rest of society and on government. They are the basic actors.

Yet it is not always easy to render an accurate and balanced description of the constellation of groups operating in any given conflict area. This is especially true of the politics of church and state, where one can find out a great deal about some of the group actors and very little about others. Groups have quite different styles. Some operate almost exclusively in public settings—court rooms, hearing rooms and news conferences; others prefer unpublicized conversations with governmental officials or other group elites. Some groups are frank and open about their aims, support and strategies; others evince a sort of institutional paranoia in their desire to keep their operations a secret.

What follows is only as a rough guide to church-state interest groups.

SEPARATIONIST GROUPS

The separationist landscape is variegated. A number of organized groups—Protestant, Jewish, secularist—reflect the various separationist ideologies, and groups with related interests (such as public education) intervene from time to time as separationist actors.

The National Council of Churches

Perhaps the most striking characteristic of Protestantism in America has been its diversity. There are many different "brands," and the centrifugal tendencies inherent in American Protestantism have made it difficult for the various denominations to cooperate effectively. Perhaps the most successful political interest group to grow out of American Protestantism was the Anti-Saloon League. But the League was a tightly organized and highly professional organization quite separate from the churches and denominational bodies. It directed its appeal to Protestants, but it was not a creation of churches acting in concert.[1]

The National Council of Churches of Christ in the U.S.A. (NCC) began life in 1908 as the "Federal" Council, and reorganized with a broader membership and the stronger title "National" in 1950. It was conceived as an agency for cooperative action on social and political matters of concern to Protestants, but it has had to battle constantly against the suspicions of fiercely independent member denominations. Today it is a somewhat uneasy alliance of Protestant and Orthodox bodies (claiming a total of 42 million members) which are represented on a General Board which approves all Council policy and budgeting. Member denominations are in no way bound by the positions taken by the Council (the Council is said to speak *to* the member denominations, not *for* them), and the Council is still anathema to many elements within the Protestant community. The National Association of Evangelicals was created, in part, as a fundamentalist alternative to what was regarded as the "modernism" of the NCC. Still other Protestant bodies find any formalized association incompatible with their institutions or creeds and they remain in splendid isolation, uncontaminated by the errors and heresies of others.

Thus when the NCC speaks it is with something less than the voice of American Protestantism. Although it includes the most prestigious denominations (often described by the adjective "old-line"), and can draw upon the services of prominent Protestant clergy and laymen, it

suffers as a political actor because of the fragmented and quarrelsome
nature of its constituency. In January 1964, for example, the General
Convention of the Protestant Episcopal Church (one of the most important NCC members) cleared the Council of charges of communism,
but reproved it for making "too many authoritative comments on social issues."[2] Such declarations of confidence scarcely add to the political leverage which NCC seeks to exercise in the political process. As
former NCC staff member Murray Stedman notes,

> Most of the largest Protestant denominations that are members of
> the NCC have offices of some sort in Washington. . . . In addi-
> tion—and it is a most serious addition—denominations which are not
> members of the NCC . . . have headquarters in Washington.
> It is easy to sympathize with the young lawyer for a government
> regulatory agency who spent his first day on the job trying to find
> out for his superior "Protestant reaction" to the draft of a proposed
> regulation. "Sir," he is said to have reported grimly, "I can find lots
> of Protestants in this city, but I'm afraid I can't give you *a* Prot-
> estant reaction." The official was not in the least perturbed. "All
> right," he said, "in that case call up my pastor. We'll simply as-
> sume his reaction is typical."[3]

Within the Council, the politics of church and state is the responsibility of the Commission on Religious Liberty. This is a grand title
for a small office headed by the Reverend Dean M. Kelley. Kelley
operates on a budget of around $40,000 per year, but he and his
predecessors have been among the most respected and effective church-
state professionals. The Commission's principal activity is lobbying at
the national level. Although it has become increasingly interested in
litigation as a means of advancing its goals (it has submitted *amicus
curiae* briefs in several important cases), the lion's share of Kelley's
time and money is spent in direct communication with national
decision-makers, in working out or establishing common positions and
approaches with other groups, and in developing propaganda intended
to convey to his targets the impression of an aroused Protestant
community.

While his budget is small, Kelley is able to call upon considerable
assistance. The NCC maintains a Washington office, and other elements
of the main secretariat, the "Protestant Vatican" at 475 Riverside Drive
in New York, can make available specialists in fields such as public
relations and statistics. He can enlist some very important Protestants
in his cause, and it is no small advantage to be able to brief an Arthur
Fleming (former Secretary of Health, Education and Welfare and now

President of the University of Oregon) or a Eugene Carson Blake (a President of the World Council of Churches) to make the NCC presentation before a congressional committee. In addition, Kelley has benefited from the services of volunteer associates such as Professor George R. La Noue of Teachers College, Columbia University, a political scientist and one of the most knowledgeable men in the country on church-state matters.

Perhaps the most significant of Kelley's accomplishments has been establishing communications among a number of the leading separationist groups. In early 1964, as the Johnson Administration was preparing the legislative proposals which became the Economic Opportunity Act of 1964, rumors circulated that some of the new programs might be implemented in part through religious institutions. Faced with the possibility of major federal funds flowing to religious institutions (those were the days when it seemed likely that the War on Poverty would ultimately involve massive spending), Kelley brought together an informal "Church-State Consortium" which included representatives of the American Jewish Congress, the American Jewish Committee, the Anti-Defamation League of B'nai B'rith, the Civil Liberties Union, the Baptist Joint Committee on Public Affairs, and the United Presbyterians. Partly through the efforts of the Consortium, the architects of the poverty proposals were persuaded to cut back somewhat on participation of religious institutions and provide safeguards which, while not regarded by the Consortium members as adequate, were better than nothing.

Finding the Consortium a useful forum for the exchange of intelligence and the development of coordinated strategies, the participants agreed to continue with Kelley as the "convener" and secretary-chairman. As we shall see, the Consortium has not only served as the instrument of communication between separationist groups, but has, on occasion, provided participating groups with a single voice in situations where quick contact and decision-making was required. Kelley, of course, holds no general warrant to speak for the Consortium and has only served as its spokesman on occasions when delegations have been dispatched to meet with government officials. Also, there are severe limits on the coordination and division of labor which are possible when the participating group representatives must satisfy their own particular constituencies, raise money on their own records of political performance, and satisfy their own egos. Nonetheless, the Consortium probably increases the effectiveness of the separationist groups which operate through it. It certainly increases Kelley's stature. Although he cannot manipulate it, the fact remains that he occupies the crucial position in the communications net. This does not go unnoticed by those in the government with whom he deals.

Thus with all its problems the NCC is the closest thing to a voice of the Protestant "establishment," and Kelley is the closest approximation to an official Protestant spokesman on church-state affairs. The organization takes a moderate-separationist stance. It is determined that there will be no direct public aid to religious institutions, but it is prepared to consider marginal compromises on indirect aid (e.g., health services in church schools).

Americans United

Protestants and Other Americans United for the Separation of Church and State (AU) was founded in 1947 as a result of the postwar rise in Protestant-Catholic hostilities noted in Chapter I. In the words of its President (and past President of the Southern Baptist Convention), Louie D. Newton, Americans United

> was shocked into existence. Bishops of the largest denomination in the United States, the Roman Catholic, had denounced Separation of Church and State as the "shibboleth of doctrinaire secularism." They summoned their people to work "patiently, persistently and perseveringly" for its destruction.[4]

Originally, this group was a coalition of liberal and conservative churchmen. These included Methodist Bishop G. Bromley Oxnam, one of the best known liberal Protestants, Paul Blanshard, also a political liberal and scathing critic of Roman Catholicism, and Clyde Taylor, Secretary of the National Association of Evangelicals and an impeccably conservative Protestant. Over the years, the organization has swung gradually to the right, both politically and theologically, until today it essentially reflects the dogmatic separationism of conservative Protestantism. Southern Baptists, Methodists, "Southern" Presbyterians, Adventists, and Evangelicals predominate within its secretariat.

The political style of Americans United is uncompromisingly militant. Its house organ, the monthly *Church and State Review*, is repetitiously hard hitting, and has been called anti-Catholic. Its lobbying at the national level (headquarters in Washington, D.C.) is intermittent and, because of this, largely ineffectual. It has relied heavily on litigation. Its Executive Director is a lawyer who keeps at least one other lawyer on his staff. AU goes to law, however, more for the sake of dramatic effect and the stimulation of separationist sentiment than to make precedents and affect the development of legal rules. Its propaganda activities are far flung, and while it did not officially oppose John F. Kennedy's candidacy for President in 1960, its literature and "Questions for Catholic Candidates" were widely distributed in the key primary states of Wisconsin and West Virginia.

AU's verbal excesses have caused some commentators to make fun of it and discount it as a serious political force. This is a mistake. Under its financially shrewd Executive Director, Glen Archer, the organization has grown from a shoestring venture in 1948 (with office space borrowed from the Baptist Joint Committee) into a large establishment with a budget of well over half a million dollars per year. Other groups which we shall examine have larger budgets, but spend only portions of them on church-state matters. Archer manages a professional staff of over twenty and a large clerical staff. A large new Washington headquarters building is on the way.

Americans United now has approximately 200,000 members who receive its publications, and maintains small regional offices in New York, Chicago, and Los Angeles. It enjoys strength and prestige in sectors of the Protestant community (Baptist and Evangelical) which are growing rapidly. Theodore Sorensen's memoirs indicate that the Kennedy staff regarded the group as having political significance. John Kennedy's comment at the 1958 Gridiron Club dinner was an indirect indication of this concern:

> Should I be elected, I do hope that Bishop Bromley Oxnam of the POAU will be my personal envoy to the Vatican—and he is instructed to open negotiations for that transatlantic tunnel immediately.[5]

Americans United has not enjoyed good relations with its natural group allies. A "more-separationist-than-thou" attitude toward friends, and a weakness for some of the classical themes and catchwords of No-Popery have damaged the group's reputation. The amount of money it has to spend causes other separationists to look longingly from time to time, but most do not want to risk the loss of prestige which might be the cost of open alliance. Only after protracted debate was AU admitted to the separationist Consortium. Needless to say, its separationism is of the strictest sort.

The Baptist Joint Committee on Public Affairs

The Baptist Joint Committee was established in 1941. In 1946 it opened an office in Washington as spokesman for four Baptist conventions (including the American and the Southern), and now includes eight Baptist groups whose combined membership is over twenty-two million. The Joint Committee was headed for fifteen years by a peppery Texas minister named Joseph Martin Dawson, who directed a small staff and kept his constituency informed of what was happening at the national governmental level which might affect the interests of Baptists. He developed a reputation as a man who knew his Baptists, and he enjoyed excellent connections on Capitol Hill. Dawson was also one of the founders of Americans United, and served as its part-time director until Glen Archer was brought in to head the group. For years the Joint Committee cooperated closely with AU, but while the latter waxed large and well funded, it never acquired the Washington prestige of the older operation.

On Dawson's retirement in 1960, the leadership of the BJC was assumed by the Reverend C. Emmanuel Carlson, who has performed as effectively as his predecessor. Carlson has been building bridges of cooperation with the NCC, taking a part in the Consortium and becoming known around Washington as a separationist moderate. Until 1963, Carlson was a member of the Board of Trustees of Americans United. Since his resignation, the Joint Committee has veered away from its erstwhile organizational protégé.

The Religious Liberty Association

A small but vigorous separationist group is the Religious Liberty Association (RLA). With a membership of 70,000 and a staff of three, RLA reflects the sensitivity of Seventh Day Adventists (as Sabbatarians, vegetarians and conscientious objectors) to questions involving religion and the public order. The RLA supports litigation in defense of Adventists, and in the case of *Sherbert v. Verner*[6] secured an important Supreme Court statement on the extent to which a state can, in pursuit of some otherwise legitimate secular purpose, place a person at a disadvantage because of his religion. South Carolina required that anyone receiving unemployment compensation accept any job offered or be declared ineligible. An Adventist refused a job which required work on Saturday, her Sabbath, and was dropped from the unemployment rolls. The Court held that the religious scruple involved was too important for the state to ignore, and that the state might protect its interests in other ways. While some might ask whether creating a religious exemption to an otherwise valid rule was not a violation of separation, the RLA does take the strict separationist line on government financial aid to religious institutions.

In addition to litigation, the RLA carries on an active propaganda program, publishing among other things a monthly glossy magazine called *Liberty*. Many of its materials are critical of Roman Catholicism, and it cooperates closely with Americans United. RLA participates in the Consortium through its director, Melvin Adams.

The American Jewish Congress

The American Jewish Congress (AJCongress) was organized in 1918 with the immediate purpose of representing American Jewish opinion at the Paris Peace Conference. Originally a holding company of Jewish organizations, it is now a membership corporation which claims about 300,000 (although the number of active members is much smaller). Since World War II it has broadened its interests from specifically Jewish problems to embrace a wide range of civil liberties and civil rights issues. It has been especially concerned with church-state matters and takes a separationist line.

The annual income of the organization is around $1 million and something over $100,000 is allocated to the Commission on Law and Social Action, which handles an extensive program of litigation. With four full-time lawyers, this office also avails itself of the services of volunteer counsel—unlike Americans United which hires its local lawyers. By far the most important resource of the Commission, especially as regards church-state and free-exercise matters, is Mr. Leo Pfeffer—one of the most knowledgeable and experienced church-state lawyers in the country. Pfeffer's books, articles and briefs constitute the most polished expression of the strict separationist constitutional position. For years the director of the Commission, Pfeffer is now chairman of the Political Science Department at Long Island University and continues as Special Counsel to the Congress. This enables him to perform as consultant on church-state cases in progress.

Although the Congress engages in research, propaganda and direct communication with legislative and executive decision-makers, the spearhead of its program is the legal work of the Commission. Its legal strategy (again, unlike that of Americans United) emphasizes the establishment of precedents. Will Maslow, Executive Director of the Congress, has stated that "we usually strive for a decision in the Su-

preme Court of the United States,"[7] and the organization, often through
Leo Pfeffer, has been involved in many of the notable recent cases involving religion and the public order.

The appeal of the AJCongress is to the Jewish middle class, and its
style is militantly liberal. Despite its combativeness, however, it has
by and large avoided charges of anti-Catholicism. It enjoys good relations with other separationist and liberal groups, especially the Civil
Liberties Union. Joseph Robison, present Director of the Commission
on Law and Social Action, represents the Congress within the separationist Consortium.

The American Jewish Committee

Founded in 1906, in reaction to the Kishiner pogroms in Russia, the
American Jewish Committee (AJCommittee) has its roots in the elite
of the Jewish community. With approximately 33,000 members in
1964, its governing bodies include some of the most wealthy and prestigious American Jews.

The Committee eschews the militant techniques of the Congress, and
its public pronouncements lack the strident and aggressive tones of the
larger (but not richer) group. The Committee often operates through
quiet personal contacts with influential decision-makers, where its impact derives from the social prominence of its leaders. The Committee
secretariat, however, does engage in lobbying, and it has financed extensive research into patterns of intergroup relations in the United
States. In addition, it cooperates in the legal work of the Anti-Defamation League.

Less outspokenly liberal than the Congress, the Committee tends to
focus more narrowly on problems of religious discrimination and
bigotry. Also, the Committee is less strictly separationist than the Congress (although not as moderate as the NCC). Its legal counsel, Ed-
win J. Lukas, is a participant in the Consortium.

The Anti-Defamation League

The Anti-Defamation League (ADL) was founded in 1913 to combat anti-semitism. It is supported by the Jewish fraternal organization
B'nai B'rith, and like the AJCongress it has expanded its interests to
include political issues and human relations far removed from the
original concern of policing discrimination against the Jews. In fact,
with an annual budget of around $4,000,000, home offices in New

York, 26 regional offices, and 200 employees, it is the largest and best financed bill-of-rights organization in the country. Recently, it has become deeply involved in the problems of open housing.

ADL takes an active interest in church-state relations, and its separationism is of the strict-to-moderate AJCommittee brand. While ADL lobbies in the church-state area and participates in the Consortium, it has not litigated church-state questions as vigorously as the AJCongress. There has, in fact, been occasional friction between the organizations over whether it was wise to "go to law" in particular situations. The ADL, with its B'nai B'rith antennae at the community level, has sometimes argued that the community tensions (and especially the anti-semitism) which would be stirred up by a church-state suit would cancel out the legal gains. The AJCongress scorns such inhibition. Nonetheless, the ADL has church-state suits on its docket, and its chief counsel, Sol Rabkin, cooperates with Pfeffer and the Congress.

The American Civil Liberties Union

Founded to combat the excesses of bigotry and repression spawned by World War I, the American Civil Liberties Union (ACLU) reported an income in 1967 of approximately two million dollars and a membership of 115,000. It is certainly the best known bill-of-rights group and probaby the most effective. While the ADL has more money, and the AJCongress claims more members, no other organization (excepting the Negro-rights groups) has succeeded in marshaling such talent or in staying so consistently on the leading edge of innovation in civil liberties law. The Union is federal in form with all contributions and dues divided between the national Union and various state affiliates. While the distinction between national and subnational is more important in this case than it is with most political interest groups (which tend to be federal on paper but centralized in fact), there is great coordination and cooperation between the national office and the affiliates.

The ACLU is also unusual in the degree to which part-time volunteers are involved in its operation. It is able to do a remarkable amount of litigating, in all sorts of civil rights and civil liberties areas, because of the large number of lawyers who contribute time and skills. In addition, policy is set by committees of part-timers, and although the full-time staff sets the agenda of the committee meetings, it seems that the members, men of high professional prominence and prestigious institutional associations, retain substantial control over the internal decisional process. The membership tends to be upper middle class, highly educated and politically liberal.

On the issues of church and state, the Union has taken a strict separationist line, despite the presence of a distinguished Jesuit on its policy-making Church-State Committee. It is tougher than NCC, and closer to the AJCongress. The Union lobbies actively at the national level, and increasingly, through its affiliates, in state capitals. While litigation remains its principal stock in trade, it has recently established a tax-exempt arm, the Roger Baldwin Foundation, to sponsor civil liberties research, and it keeps its position before the public by conventional propaganda techniques. The Union has managed or contributed to many of the most important church-state cases of the past decade, and participates in the separationist Consortium through Lawrence Speiser, Director of its Washington office. At a rough estimate, ten to twenty percent of the Union's substance and energy is devoted to the politics of church and state.

Educational Groups

Strictly speaking, these groups are not church-state professionals, but their ubiquity in struggles over public aid to church-related schools requires that they be mentioned. Their commitment to the separation of church and state is a function of their commitment to the cause of public education, and they have recently shown what separationist purists consider a distressing willingness to forget about church-state considerations when substantial amounts of money for public schools are at stake. Nonetheless, educational groups are politically powerful, and they have traditionally thrown their weight against the religious educators whom they have regarded as natural enemies.*

---

*What seems to be happening, and what the separationist purists regard as sinister, is a growing perception on the part of public school partisans that their traditional conception of the competition between themselves and religious educators is wrong. Given the configuration of political forces in America today, they are not involved in a zero-sum game (in which what one side wins the other side loses), but in a non-zero-sum game (in which all players can win something without arithmetically reducing each others' winnings). There is no fixed resource "pie" from which the church-related schools will or will not get a piece; rather, the size and availability of pie (special sorts of aid for education) will depend on what sharing arrangements can be worked out among the claimants. The non-zero-sum game invites cooperation between the players, and as this realization spreads among public schoolmen, separationists can expect more defections.

By far the most important group is the National Education Association (NEA). Founded in 1857, NEA has over a million members today, and is the nearest thing to an inclusive organization of school teachers in America. The group's reputation for effectiveness as a Washington lobbyist is high, and until the 1960's the United States Office of Education was regarded by many as an NEA fief. The recent drawing away of the Office from the Association has been traumatic, and has brought down the wrath of NEA on the successive Commissioners of Education since 1961. President Kennedy's first commissioner, Dr. Sterling M. McMurrin, was an especial target, and he later described NEA as suffering from bigness and as "too much involved in perpetuating the status quo in education."[8]

Other educational groups which have adopted separationist positions include the American Association of School Administrators, the Council of Chief State School Officers, the American Federation of Teachers (AFL–CIO), the American Council on Education and the Horace Mann League. All of these are active lobbies, and the Horace Mann League has been the official sponsor of one of the most important church-state cases in recent years. No educational group participates regularly in the work of the Consortium, but their representatives have occasionally been invited to sit in.

It should not be assumed from this lumping together of educational groups that they always take the same positions—even on aid to church-related schools. The School Administrators are suspicious of both the NEA (teachers) and State School Officers (state commissioners). In our examination of church-state conflict in New York (Chapter IV), we shall see an interesting split between the local school administrators and state educational officials over an issue of government aid to church-related schools.

Separationist Miscellany

The NCC, AU, and the Baptist Joint Committee have established themselves as the major Protestant voices in the area of church and state, but a number of other Protestant organizations, often possessing substantial numbers and prestige, intervene from time to time. The Board of Christian Social Concerns of the Methodist Church, the National Affairs Office of the United Presbyterians (a denomination which formally reaffirmed a strict separationist policy several years ago), the Unitarian-Universalist Association and the Council for Christian Social Action of the United Church of Christ are among the many

Protestant agencies which issue occasional statements and present testimony at legislative hearings. The Masons, especially those of the Scottish Rite, have also taken separationist action from time to time. The Scottish Rite provided the original funds which launched Americans United in 1948, and individual lodges and Masons have figured in many AU law suits and other battles as financial supporters, local counsel and after-dinner speakers.

Jewish "denominational" bodies, such as the Union of American Hebrew Congregations (Reform), also participate in this intermittent fashion, as does the American Humanist Association. In the past the AFL–CIO has occasionally lent support to the separationist position, as have Americans for Democratic Action (ADA), and the American Veterans Committee. The most significant recent recruits to the ranks of part-time separationists, as we have noted, have been the Negro rights groups. In addition, there are a few New York City groups whose prominence has so increased because of recent local battles that they have begun to establish themselves as separationist voices in Washington. These include the Protestant Council of the City of New York, the United Parents Association, the Public Education Association and the United Federation of Teachers (a local of the American Federation of Teachers, AFL–CIO).

One more class of separationist organizations must be mentioned—those which Ralph Lord Roy has called the "apostles of discord."[9] These supposedly Protestant groups constitute an underworld of bigotry which is nativistic and anti-Catholic in the worst traditions of 19th-century No-Popery. Many of these are one-man operations. They may be led by a charlatan or a fanatic but in either case the groups are pernicious. They tend to be separationist only on aid to parochial schools, and favor publicly sponsored religious exercises. It is difficult to assess their political significance. While their immediate impact on the policy-making process is certainly slight, the extent of their followings and potential audience is unknown. Hopefully they can be written off as curiosities, but the possibility cannot be ignored that by feeding the ancient fires of xenophobic anti-Catholicism these groups retard cultural change and thus have an indirect political impact.

ACCOMMODATIONIST GROUPS

Cognoscentes of New York City politics often refer to the Chancellery of the Archdiocese of New York, headed for so long by the late Francis Cardinal Spellman, as "The Powerhouse." It is reputed to be a constant and influential actor across a wide range of municipal issues from street closings (the Archdiocese is a large property owner) to welfare (opposition to birth control services). Unfortunately there are no doctoral dissertations or learned articles which afford specification and documentation of these assertions. The Chancellery's influence is undoubtedly real, but it is usually exercised in nonpublic forums. Invisibility, in turn, breeds legend and exaggeration.[10]

Precisely this problem is involved in introducing and describing the accommodationist actors in the politics of church and state. With the marked exception of Citizens for Educational Freedom, which might almost be said to have adopted a "separationist style," the accommodationists work quietly and rely heavily on negotiations at the top. Representatives of the U.S. Catholic Conference do testify before committees and issue public statements, and individual members of the hierarchy take positions openly. In addition, the few Jewish accommodationists are quite vocal. On the whole, however, the accommodationist side of the stage is more muted than the separationist, and the risks for the analyst are proportionally increased.

The Catholic Hierarchy

There is a widespread impression among non-Catholics that the Catholic Church in the United States is a highly integrated and monolithic organization capable of rapid and disciplined mobilization from the top downward. Catholic commentators find this amusing and often wish it were so. The fact is that, however much discipline and conformity may exist within a particular diocese, each diocese is directed by its own bishop. The bishop is an independent actor owing obedience to no authority save the Pope, and to him on only a shrinking number of matters. Catholic bishops are the last of the great autocrats. Not even the business world, where the individual entrepreneur is increasingly replaced by the organizational team, offers many examples of the sort of autonomy enjoyed by these spiritual leaders.

The ideological homogeneity and the common social and political experience of the American Catholic community (and its predominantly Irish priesthood) tend to obscure from non-Catholics the simple fact that the Church in the United States is a collection of baronies.[11] There is no head of the American Church. Certainly the Catholic community is much better organized than the Protestant community, possessing better channels of internal communication through its diocesan press and numbers of specialized associations. But this is not to say much. Traditionally, the Vatican has discouraged the development of any intervening authority between it and the individual bishops. From the time of the Conciliar Movement in the Middle Ages until quite recently, attempts at organization among the bishops of any country have been regarded as threats to the Pope's primacy in ecclesiastical affairs.

The American bishops are often involved in politics. But when one speaks of the "hierarchy intervening" in a political conflict, one usually means that Bishop X has intervened or that an informal alliance of Bishop X and three others has become involved. Obviously Catholic bishops do not always intervene on the same issues or with the same style. There are some bishops still doing battle against birth control, and some dioceses where contraception is regarded as a matter of private morality rather than a public issue. One should not assume that because American Catholics almost unanimously support public aid to parochial schools there is a master plan going forward to achieve this end. As we shall see, the bishops have developed a national secretariat to articulate Catholic views in the high councils of Washington D.C., and similar agencies have been created at the state level. But while this national organization has begun to assume episcopal responsibilities, it is a long way from being a comprehensive planning structure for the Catholic Church in the United States.

Individual priests, bishops and cardinals are often men of considerable community-wide or national prestige; they take on added political potential from the fact that they are thought to be on very special terms with the voters who are their spiritual charges. The "special relationship" which traditionally has existed between the Catholic clergy and the Democratic Party organizations in many cities increases this potential. Taking the hierarchy together, it probably constitutes the most important accommodationist "actor." But it is a strange kind of composite actor, with multiple faces, interests and degrees of participation.

The United States Catholic Conference

The United States Catholic Conference (USCC) is the instrument by which the bishops have attempted to overcome fragmentation, localism and lack of coordination. Although it cannot issue any orders on social or political matters, it serves as an agency for the expression of carefully hammered-out policy statements and is currently adding to its influence and jurisdiction.

The organization (until 1966 the National Catholic Welfare Conference) had its beginning during World War I in a group established at the initiative of Cardinal Gibbons to watch over the interests of Catholic servicemen. This experiment in cooperation among bishops proved so encouraging that it was decided to continue it after 1918 in order to "organize Roman Catholic activities in education, social welfare, immigrant aid, and youth guidance," and to provide a central secretariat for the bishops. Until recently, the whole organization rested on the willingness of individual bishops to participate. No one needed to have anything to do with the NCWC, and it had no power to bind clergy or laymen to its positions. However, this may be changing. The Conference was reorganized in 1966, after a softening of Rome's opposition to national Catholic formations was signaled at Vatican II, and the way was opened for a college of American bishops exercising some ecclesiastical authority.

Before 1966 the bishops had met each fall in a nameless caucus presided over by the senior cardinal. This meeting chose an Administrative Board of ten bishops (with the cardinals acting ex officio) to oversee the work of the Conference secretariat. At its November 1966 meeting, the caucus gave itself a name (the National Conference of Catholic Bishops), elected a president (the Most Reverend John Francis Dearden, Archbishop of Detroit), and announced that it would henceforth function in a more active leadership capacity for the American Catholic community. It is establishing jurisdiction over certain liturgical matters, and plans to establish a theological and canonical commission. Clearly this assumption of ecclesiastical powers has the potential of strengthening the Conference as a political actor. The secretariat of the USCC—the full-time professionals who do the actual work of the organization—will continue to be supervised by an administrative board elected by the bishops. It is quartered in Washington, D.C. and is large, well financed and functionally organized. The most important departments for the politics of church and state are those of law and education.

The education department, under the leadership of its late director, Monsignor Frederick G. Hochwalt, led the accommodationist fight against President Kennedy's federal aid to education proposals in 1961 and 1962 (these excluded church schools) and it has played an important part in the continuous struggle over the administration of President Johnson's Elementary and Secondary Education Act of 1965. The National Catholic Educational Association (14,000 teachers and administrators) is closely associated with the USCC, and for years Monsignor Hochwalt served as its executive secretary. This interlocking directorate has made for excellent communication and coordination within the Catholic educational establishment.

The legal department, headed by a layman, William Considine, does not go into court, but has been an active source of legal advice to accommodationists who are involved in litigation. Staffed with five full-time lawyers, it also has the principal responsibility for USCC lobbying. It was the legal department which arranged for the publication, during the heat of the 1961 Kennedy education battle, of a detailed brief setting forth the NCWC position on the constitutionality of public aid to sectarian schools. This was in answer to an administration brief (prepared in the office of the legal counsel of the Department of Health, Education, and Welfare) which argued the unconstitutionality of such aid. These have become bench-mark documents in the debates over interpretation of the religious clauses of the First Amendment.[12]

Students of political interest groups are fond of observing that such organizations tend to be directed by their secretariats with members and boards of trustees easily persuaded and swept along. This does not seem to be true of USCC. Certainly the full-time professionals who man the secretariat favor particular policy positions and attempt to persuade the bishops of the administrative board to adopt them. Unless the USCC is quite unlike similarly constructed organizations, there is some scrambling on the part of factions within the secretariat to curry special favor with the bishops. Yet with all this, the bishops retain a high degree of control over the full-time establishment. While there is no study of the NCWC to shed light on the problem, it is pardonable to speculate that the high "deference value" of the bishops, and the importance which they place on their work, have something to do with keeping the professionals in a more subordinate status than is usual. In this one respect, the USCC bears an interesting resemblance to the American Civil Liberties Union.

Little Catholic conferences have been organized in various states. New York's is directed by a contentious layman named Charles Tobin, who has recently been in the thick of battles over birth control, divorce reform, abortion law reform and aid to church-related schools.

Citizens for Educational Freedom

Citizens for Educational Freedom (CEF) is a major new accommodationist actor. It was founded in 1959 at St. Louis, at the initiative of the Reverend Virgil Blum, S.J., a political scientist at Marquette University, and has since waxed strong. In 1964 it moved its headquarters to Washington. It desires full public support for church schools. Open to adherents of all faiths, the group now claims over 128,000 members and, like its single-purpose separationist counterpart, Americans United, CEF operates on a budget of well over half a million dollars.

While CEF's membership is probably around 90 percent Catholic, it is a determinedly lay operation. It is neither the direct instrument of any bishop nor indirectly controlled through the USCC. In fact, CEF's relations with official Catholicism have not been untroubled. The notion of laymen participating in an important way to win support for parochial schools does not appeal to the more conservative of Catholic educators. After all, if laymen are instrumental in achieving aid, they may also claim an active part in running the schools which benefit from the new support. In addition, CEF has been considerably more militant and uncompromising in its advocacy than has most of the hierarchy and the Catholic Conference. There have been grumblings in high places that the new group may actually set the cause back by pushing too hard.

CEF claims to be organized down to the state and local levels, and although this organization is undoubtedly spotty (the claim of 1000 chapters in 50 states must be severely discounted), it has shown greater capacity than any other professional church-state group to operate in state legislatures and to intervene in electoral campaigns. It has spearheaded successful drives for bus transportation for parochial school students in several states, most notably in Wisconsin in the spring of 1967. Its litigation consists mostly of defensive actions, submitting *amicus curiae* briefs in support of challenged statutes and practices which it approves.

CEF's calls for accommodation are phrased in apocalyptic terms and assert that the survival of "God-centered" education in America is at stake. It reasons that schools today are becoming dependent for excellence on new sources of finance, especially federal aid. It is not only that costs of maintaining old things (buildings and teachers) will continue to rise, but that new indiciae of excellence (closed-circuit TV, computers and teaching machines) will be tremendously expensive. While the organization refrains from outright advocacy of federal aid to education, it does take the position that independent schools must share equally in all new funding. If this is not done, CEF concludes, it will mean the slow death of God-centered schools in America, and

a substantial reduction in the capacity for the free exercise of religion
by millions of citizens.

The Christianity and Crisis *Connection*

Though small in number, one of the most important accommodationist groups is an informal group of liberal Protestant clergymen, many
of whom are connected with Union Theological Seminary and write for
the journal *Christianity and Crisis.* Moving spirits of this little band
are Reinhold Niebuhr, the eminent Protestant theologian and social
critic, and John C. Bennett, the President of Union Seminary.

These men are convinced that there is considerable justice in the
claims of Catholic educators, and are especially concerned for the future of religious training in America. At a time when a tide of indifference seems to be eroding the foundations of Christianity—when
theistic religion seems to be declining as a force in the culture—they
find it foolish for Christians to squabble over what they regard as the
outworn values of strict separation. Dr. Bennett has gone so far as to
declare that there *is* no Protestant doctrine of the separation of church
and state—realizing that if you can get enough people to ignore an
idea, it goes away.[13] On both public prayer and aid to denominational
schools the group tends to advocate governmental action to favor religion as long as no one's free exercise is impaired.

This informal group has no programs of the kind carried out by the
organized groups which we have been discussing, but it is composed of
prestigious Protestants. What they write and say in public forums
counts for much, and they are occasionally invited by legislative committees and other official bodies to give testimony as independent ex-
perts on church-state relations. Most importantly, however, they offer
accommodationists the opportunity of pointing to prominent friends in
the Protestant community.

Jewish Newcomers

Orthodox Jews have been in the independent school business for
some time, and with a recent quickened development of Jewish day
schools in major metropolitan areas, significant numbers of middle-
class Jews are availing themselves of nonpublic educational options
for their children. Something like a Jewish private educational establishment has come into existence, and it is no wonder that the prospect
of new educational financing—federal and state aid—has brought accommodationist stirrings within this element of the Jewish community.

Agudath Israel, a defense organization for Orthodox Judaism, and the National Jewish Commission on Law and Public Affairs, an organization of lawyers and social scientists, have been the principal spokesmen for Orthodox views. Individual Jewish educators, such as Arnold Brickman of the University of Pennsylvania, have lent their support to aid to sectarian schools, and the Jewish counterpart of Protestant accommodationist Reinhold Niebuhr is the theologian and publicist Will Herberg. His writings in favor of aid to church-related schools and of prayers in public schools are widely quoted in accommodationist circles. The Jewish day schools are directly represented by the National Society for Hebrew Day Schools.

It is clear that these are the voices of only a small minority of American Jews. But, while it seems unlikely that the accommodationists will seriously challenge the dominant separationist groups for leadership of Jewish opinion, they may continue to grow modestly and generate considerable debate within the Jewish community. Their existence is an excellent example of the way in which the spread of nonpublic education makes accommodationists.

Accommodationist Miscellany

The Knights of Columbus (K of C) was founded in 1882 as a Catholic alternative to the Odd Fellows, Elks and other life-insurance-and-good-fellowship societies which were becoming popular. With 1,165,500 members and over $25,000,000 in real estate holdings, the K of C will occasionally finance church-state litigation. (It helped pay the costs of *Pierce v. Society of Sisters*,[14] which in 1925 established the right of non-public schools to exist.) While leaving day-to-day Washington lobbying to the USCC, the Knights are often on the list to testify at hearings involving aid to church-related schools. Although the K of C's intervention into politics have sometimes been a trifle bumptious, it has deep extensive roots in the Catholic community, it can write a big check and it is often on very good terms with local Democratic party influentials.

To a somewhat lesser extent, groups representing Catholic lawyers, Catholic veterans, and Catholic teachers speak out and propagandize for the accommodationist cause. At the very fringe of accommodationism are groups such as organized police and firemen. Often with heavily Catholic memberships, they stand ready to deplore Supreme Court decisions banning public prayer and applaud the work of church-related schools. There are, of course, certain fundamentalist Protestant bodies which also favor public prayer, but as they definitely do not favor aid to religion or religious institutions they cannot really be classed as accommodationist.

COMPARISONS

Comparing the two sets of actors, it appears that most separationist groups are prominent in what journalists are fond of calling the Liberal Establishment (conservative Protestant groups such as AU and the fundamentalist formations are glaring exceptions). This is the network of labor, religious, civil rights and reformist interests which provide crucial support for federal innovation in race relations, welfare and education. These include the AFL–CIO,* the National Council of Churches, ADA, the Civil Liberties Union and the Negro rights groups. The accommodationists, while not uniformly conservative, are not a part of this constellation of reformist forces. The contrast is apparent in the House of Representatives where separationists tend to have high access to young liberals from competitive districts, and the accommodationists have high access to old-style organization politicals from relatively safe districts (Hugh Carey of Brooklyn and John McCormack of South Boston are cases in point). It is characteristic of the politics of church and state that "reform" has a separationist allegiance, and "the machine" tends toward accommodation. This seems to be a reflection of both ideology (liberals tend to be secularist and Jeffersonian) and ethnic politics (old-line organization pols tend to be Catholic). Like most generalizations about Congress, this one must be bent to take care of the South. There are a number of separationist Baptists holding down safe Southern seats, and here conservative Protestant separationists enjoy high access. Nevertheless, the overall pattern is clear enough to be worthy of note.

---

*Although increasing doubt is expressed by separationist and Negro spokesmen as to whether the AFL-CIO is any longer interested in their cause.

CHAPTER THREE

THE ARENAS
OF CONFLICT

Political warfare over the relationship of church to state is waged at all levels of government and in a variety of ways—in arguments before the United States Supreme Court, at learned conferences, within committees of Congress, within local school boards and in demonstrations and picket lines. Stepping back from this canvas of activity, however, it is possible to identify three major arenas in which church-state issues are fought out: (1) the constitutional arena, (2) the national legislative-administrative arena and (3) the state-and-local arena—which includes the whole range of nonjudicial governmental units below the federal level. Important public policy adjustments are made in each arena; each requires different modes of political action and makes different demands on the political actors involved. The arenas are interrelated (particular conflicts move from one to another, and what happens in one may affect another) but possess distinct characteristics. Dividing the politics of church and state along these rather gross lines emphasizes the way in which issues are adjusted through a continuing and interconnected governmental process, and avoids the disjunctions of an analysis which strictly follows the formal structure of government—Congress, Supreme Court, state legislatures, etc.

THE CONSTITUTIONAL ARENA

In discussing constitutional politics it is a mistake to focus exclusively on the work of the courts. Constitutional controversies have important extra-judicial dimensions. For instance, a large semischolarly

literature has been developed in recent years to bolster varying inter-
pretations of the First Amendment's religion clauses. This includes
some excellent examples of the writing of history to justify particular
public policy preferences.[1] Across seminar tables and in learned jour-
nals interested parties seek to enlist the "historical Jefferson" in their
cause, or alternatively, argue that Jefferson's importance in the development of American church-state relations has been over-emphasized and
that insufficient attention has been paid to Roger Williams, George
Washington, Justice Joseph Story or whoever has written a few words
that seem to support the sort of church-state arrangement the commentator presently desires.

One example of scholarly squabbling will suffice. In 1822 Jefferson,
as rector of the University of Virginia, agreed—with considerable re-
luctance it would appear—to allow "some pious individuals . . . to
establish their religious schools on the confines of the University, so
as to give their students ready and convenient access and attendance on
the scientific lectures of the University."[2] Anyone who has attended
many discussions or debates between church-state activists knows as
soon as this quotation is mentioned that he is in for an extended exchange on the early 19th-century meaning of the word "confines."
The reverend gentleman from Fordham will contend that Jefferson
meant "on the grounds of the University." The learned gentleman
from Yale will counter that Jefferson clearly meant "off, but adjacent
to, the campus." The urbane gentleman from Harvard will suggest
that Jefferson was being deliberately ambiguous, and conclude that the
reference cannot be scored for either side. While silly on its face, such
"founding-father-splitting" has a serious aspect. The participants in
these haggles are quite aware that in the long run they will win or lose
on the public policy merits of their positions. They know they must
convince powerful people that the course of wisdom is stricter separation or greater accommodation. Yet judicial decisions, and especially
statements of the Supreme Court, are not made in an historical vacuum.
The Justices make new law, but they do not make it out of whole
cloth. The Court is constantly engaged in justifying new departures in
constitutional law in terms of the body of decisions, assumptions and
intentions which went before. There is innovation on the basis of what
the Justices believe to be sound public policy, but it is innovation within
a context of continuity. It is an obligation of the Supreme Court, crucial to its rule-adapting and tradition-maintaining functions in the
American system, that it link its doctrinal departures with the past. It

must reconcile new rules with old principles, or state clearly why the old principles were mistaken and in conflict with another more important constitutional tradition. To be able to claim "framers' intention" in support of one's constitutional preferences is never an inconsequential advantage. This is true not only when constitutional questions are being argued before courts, but also when propaganda appeals are being made to enlist support for combat in a nonconstitutional arena.

There is nothing sinister about such politically purposeful use of history. Historical materials are always inconclusive of contemporary disputes, constitutional or otherwise, and it is to be expected that all parties will make the best use of whatever ammunition they find in the American past. While little of this historical maneuvering is, strictly speaking, the work of organizations, the interest group identifications of the authors are often apparent, and their productions are eagerly seized on and used as ammunition by group leaders.

The United States Supreme Court is, of course, the most important agency within the constitutional arena. In a series of decisions, beginning with *Everson v. Board of Education*[3] in 1947, the Court has attempted to articulate a viable and principled interpretation of the First Amendment's injunction that "Congress shall make no law respecting an establishment of religion." While the Court has tended toward a strict separationist interpretation of the establishment clause, including the banning of prayer recitation and devotional Bible reading in the public schools, there are great gaps and unanswered questions in the federal constitutional law of church and state.

Less prominent than the United States Supreme Court, but often important in the constitutional politics of church and state, are the high courts of the various states. Many state constitutions have provisions dealing with public aid to religious institutions which seem, on their faces, to require strict separation. And while state courts may not allow more public aid to churches than the Supreme Court admits as constitutional on federal grounds, they may, where state money is concerned, allow less. This makes state decisions attractive to litigious separationist interest groups. If the state high court can be persuaded to decide a case on federal constitutional grounds, this increases the likelihood of United States Supreme Court review. If the decision is on state constitutional grounds it at least binds a sizable number of people. Furthermore, a strong decision on state grounds, especially if it comes from a large state, may have symbolic importance far beyond the numbers of people and the particular issue involved. The United States Supreme Court is interested not only in history, but also in the climate of reasonably informed opinion in the country. It is always possible that some state court utterance will strike one or more of the Justices as having the timbre of the vox populi.

Thus the courts, and especially the United States Supreme Court, set outer limits on what government may do, and these limitations are of crucial concern to all those involved in church-state politics. There will always be murky areas where judicial pronouncements are not clear; where legislatures, administrative agencies, school boards and community action agencies will determine the relationship of religion to the public order. And there will always be disputes over the desirability as policy of things which are clearly constitutional. Yet the continuing battle for the new constitutional law is the pivot on which the entire church-state controversy turns. Each new statement or inflection from the Supreme Court (or from a state court on a state matter) alters the context of the church-state struggle to the advantage of some groups, and feeds back into the continuing scholarly debate over what the law should be.

The Outlines of the Law

What is the present shape of the federal constitutional law of church and state? Where are its growth points, and where is scholarly and political attention focused? If we are to understand the constitutional politics of church and state, we must know something of the questions currently being raised.

The facts of the *Everson* case were simple. The State of New Jersey had authorized local school boards to reimburse parents of children attending nonpublic institutions for fares the children paid on regular bus lines in getting to and from school. The school board of the town of Ewing elected to do so, and one Arch Everson challenged the expenditures on the grounds that they violated the establishment clause. He sued as a taxpayer of Ewing—an action provided for by New Jersey law. His argument was rejected by the New Jersey courts, and ultimately the Supreme Court agreed to hear it.

In this first direct Supreme Court statement on the meaning of the establishment clause, Justice Hugo Black wrote for a majority including Justices Douglas, Reed, Murphy and Chief Justice Fred Vinson. Accepting the argument that the Fourteenth Amendment renders the establishment clause applicable to the states, Black went on to develop a strict interpretation of that requirement. "The 'establishment of religion clause' of the First Amendment," he announced, "means at least this:

> Neither a state nor the Federal Government can set up a church. Neither can pass laws which aid one religion, aid all religions, or prefer one religion over another. . . . No tax in any amount, large or small, can be levied to support any religious activity or institutions, whatever they may be called, or whatever form they may adopt to teach or practice religion. Neither a state nor the Federal Government can, openly or secretly, participate in the affairs of any religious organizations or groups and vice versa. In the words of Jefferson, the clause against any establishment of religion by law was intended to erect 'a wall of separation between church and state.' "[4]

But this was not the end of Black's opinion. After making it clear that the Constitution would tolerate no public support to religion, Black crisply concluded that no such support was involved in the New Jersey case. The beneficiaries of the aid were the children and not the schools they attended. The expenditure was not an aid to religion, but a public safety measure similar to "ordinary police and fire protection, connections for sewage disposal, public highways and sidewalks." Black did indicate that New Jersey practice was a borderline case—on the "verge" of the constitutional power of the state—but acceptable.

Four of his brethren disagreed. In a biting dissent Justice Robert Jackson likened Black to Byron's Julia who "whispering 'I will ne'er consent,'—consented." Joined by Justice Frankfurter, he rejected the distinction between the child and the school.

> It is of no importance in this situation whether the beneficiary of this expenditure of tax-raised funds is primarily the parochial school and incidentally the pupil, or whether the aid is directly bestowed on the pupil with indirect benefits to the school. The state cannot maintain a Church and it can no more tax its citizens to furnish free carriage to those who attend a Church.[5]

The Catholic parochial school, Jackson concluded, was an establishment of religion (Black himself accepted this), and to transport persons to its doors was to serve it unconstitutionally. In a second dissent Justice Wiley Rutledge, joined by Justice Burton, agreed that the indirect nature of a benefit could not legitimate it.[6]

Thus the full bench *agreed* that no aid was permissible to a religious institution, and that a school in which religion is taught along with secular subjects was such an institution. The break came and continues to come, on the question of what state action constitutes *aid*. In 1948 a majority of eight struck down a program of "released time"—time set aside within the public school day for religious instruction—where the instruction was given on public school premises. In 1952 a majority of six approved another released-time program under which children left the public school building for their religious classes.[7] In the first case aid was given because property was used; in the second case, where no property was involved, the Court found no aid. In cases in the early 1960's involving religious exercises in the public schools, the Court held that it constituted impermissible public aid to religion for the state to sponsor praying and Bible reading in schools.[8]

The "Individual-Benefit" Theory

Since 1947 the distinction between direct and indirect aid has become politically crucial. The Higher Education Facilities Construction Act of 1963, the Operation Head Start programs under the Economic Opportunity Act of 1964, and the Elementary and Secondary Education Act of 1965—three major federal innovations which involve government with religious institutions—were justified by their bureaucratic and congressional backers on the grounds that they benefit individuals and aid institutions only indirectly. No one (at least no one who is constitutionally literate) expects that the Supreme Court will approve unrestricted grants to church-related schools or other institutions which propagate religious doctrine. But on the basis of Black's *Everson* opinion a constitutional argument has been developed known as the "individual-benefit" theory—if benefit to a religious institution is only incidental to aid given an individual it is permissible. This has become the essence of the accommodationist constitutional case as it is put forward by the United States Catholic Conference and Citizens for Educational Freedom. And an additional fillip is given the accommodationist argument by the way in which its terms are defined. Accommodationist spokesmen tend to use direct and indirect as descriptions of governmental intent. Thus if the intention of the program is to help, say, school children, aid to the school must be considered indirect regardless of its practical effects. The separationists who oppose this individual-benefit argument fall into two groups: (1) those who reject the direct-indirect distinction completely, and (2) those who see it as acceptable in principle but difficult, if not impossible, of application.

Of the first group little need be said. These are the strict separationists who keep alive the constitutional views embodied in the Jackson and Rutledge dissents in *Everson,* and hope for the day when a new Supreme Court majority will firmly close the door Black left ajar. Taking this position are such groups as AU, the ACLU and the AJCongress.

The moderate separationists are willing to accept a direct-indirect distinction, but not the interpretation put on the words by accommodationists. They are prepared to live with *Everson* if careful ground rules are worked out to judge "directness" objectively—in terms of what the program at issue *does* for religious institutions. This is the approach of the National Council of Churches. La Noue, for instance, has suggested a set of guidelines for federal aid to education which have been much discussed over the past year. He would allow non-public-school students to participate in public programs of educational enrichment provided that: (1) religious institutes receive no property (neither title nor permanent possession) under the program; (2) that administration of programs remain in the hands of public officials; and (3) that there be no religious teaching or content in any of the publicly assisted programs.[9] La Noue does not believe that the present federal programs, as they have been administered, fulfill these conditions, and he is increasingly pessimistic about the long-term workability of the individual-benefit theory. The potential for abuse, he suggests, may simply be too great, and if abuse proves endemic, moderates will be driven back to the strict separationist position.[10]

All sides agree upon the need for new federal constitutional law, but given the recent performance and present composition of the Supreme Court, the separationists are somewhat more confident than the accommodationists.*

The Dirksen Amendment
Especially heartening to separationist constitutional lawyers have been the decisions in the prayer and Bible-reading cases. We have already noted that these did not touch on the distinction between direct and indirect aid, but it is necessary to pause for more careful consideration of their significance and of the various reactions they evoked.

---

* However, this confidence was dispelled on June 10, 1968, when the Court, providing the first clarification of the direct-indirect distinction since *Everson,* upheld the New York textbook loan scheme as a benefit to the child. The vote was 6-3, and the background on the case is sketched in Chapter IV.

In *Engle v. Vitale,* decided in June of 1962, a majority of seven Justices, with Black as spokesman, held that the use of a brief non-denominational prayer authorized by the Board of Regents of the State of New York for recitation in the public schools was an unconstitutional exercise of state power. It was a governmentally propagated religious exercise. In the weeks following this decision violent criticism was directed at the Court by prominent figures, both spiritual and temporal. The most colorful abuse came, as is often the case, from within Congress. Representative L. Mendel Rivers (D., S.C.) accused the Court of "legislating—they never adjudicate—with one eye on the Kremlin and the other on the National Association for the Advancement of Colored People."[11] His House colleague, Representative Frank Becker (R., N.Y.) called the decision "the most tragic in the history of the United States,"[12] and spoke of the need for a constitutional amendment to undo the mischief. Condemnation of the new ruling was widespread among religious leaders, with only a few of the most separationist Protestants and Jews supporting the Court. Francis Cardinal Spellman announced that the decision "strikes at the very heart of the Godly tradition in which America's children have for so long been raised."[13]

Anti-Court mutterings continued through the summer of 1962, but as the year closed, interest in the matter seemed to wane. In the spring of 1963, however, the Court returned to the problem of religious exercises in public schools, and in *Murray v. Curlett* and *Abington School District v. Schempp* disapproved recitation of the Lord's Prayer and Bible-reading (as a formal exercise) in public classrooms.

The 1963 reaction differed from that of 1962 in an important respect. As in 1962, there were anguished calls for constitutional amendment, but in 1963 few separationists joined in the outcry. The religious and civic leaders who rallied to the anti-Court banner were predominantly persons previously identified with the accommodationist cause; often they were spokesmen for groups actively working for more public cooperation with religious institutions. Thus Monsignor John J. Voight, Secretary for Education of the New York Archdiocese, said that the action of the court was regrettable.

> One, because it will bring about the complete secularization of public education . . . and, two, because it completely disregards parental rights in education and the wishes of a large segment of America's parents who want their children to participate in the practices in public schools.[14]

Dr. Mark Murphy, National Vice-President of Citizens for Educational Freedom, asserted that the decision established "Godless schools," and was "another step toward the elimination of God from all public American life."[15]

In the 88th, the 89th, and the 90th Congresses, amendments were proposed which would alter the establishment clause to provide for various forms of state-sponsored prayer. In the 88th, the battle for the amendment was led by Representative Becker. After 1964, the Senate minority leader, Everett McKinley Dirksen (R., Ill.), made the pro-prayer cause very much his own.

The now-familiar "Dirksen Amendment," which has twice failed of passage but which the Senator steadfastly refuses to abandon, would alter the First Amendment to provide that nothing in the Constitution shall prohibit school authorities from "providing for or permitting the voluntary participation by students or others in prayer." The significance of this proposal for the accommodationist constitutional position is clear. If religious exercises are prohibited in the public schools, and if the strictest sort of separation is required of all governmental agencies, future Supreme Court majorities will have to be very wary of governmental support of non-public institutions in which the forbidden exercises are part of the routine. But with Dirksen's language in the Constitution, it could be argued that the Federal Government was officially friendly to religion and that what goes on in church-related schools differs only in detail from constitutionally permissible public devotionals.

There is no immediate prospect of congressional approval for anything like the Dirksen Amendment, but the conflict which it has generated between accommodationist and separationist camps reveals the constitutional nuances which are the stock in trade of church-state lawyers.

The Legal Strategies

Such are the substantive issues, but knowing what the conflict is about is not the same as knowing how it is carried on. I have suggested that the politics of church and state is best understood in terms of competing interest groups, and this can be seen clearly in the constitutional arena. The battle in the courts is highly professionalized, with most of the significant church-state cases handled, in whole or in part, by the full-time legal staff and specialized volunteers of the interested organizations.[16] Arch Everson's attack against the New Jersey bus transportation law, for instance, was supported by the money and expertise of the American Civil Liberties Union. The released-time cases, although both were begun by individuals, became joint ACLU-AJCongress cases, and the school prayer cases were also group efforts backed by these two groups.

The church-state lawyers constitute a small and specialized bar; there is a high level of communication among like-minded partisans and even between separationists and accommodationists. The relationship between the Commission on Law and Social Action of the AJCongress, under the leadership of Leo Pfeffer, and the ACLU, under Patrick Murphy Malin and then John Pemberton, has been perhaps the closest and most productive alliance, but Pfeffer has also been careful to stay in close touch with other centers of activity such as the legal office of Americans United, and the office of Kenneth Greenawalt, a distinguished New York lawyer and Congregational layman who has made himself an expert on church-state law and handled cases from both the ACLU and AU. Since early 1964, the AJCongress has distributed to concerned separationists a semi-annual docket of pending church-state cases. Cases are arranged topically, and the attorneys of record and sponsoring groups are noted. In many instances local attorneys are required to submit the "papers," but the planning of the argument is done by the sponsoring group in consultation with the local man. The reproduction on the opposite page reports a typical ACLU–AJCongress case on bus transportation in which the planners hope ultimately to overturn *Everson* or at least persuade the state court to proscribe the transportation on state constitutional grounds.

The American Jewish Committee, the Anti-Defamation League, and Kelley's office at the National Council of Churches are also in close touch with the AJCongress operation, and there are many overlapping memberships in which the leaders and lawyers of the key separationist groups sit on each others' boards and steering committees. Thus Dean Kelley and George La Noue are both members of the Union's Church State Committee and Will Maslow, director of the AJCongress sits on the Union's National Board. Standing outside this interlocking directorate of separationist agencies is the Watchtower Bible and Tract Society of the Jehovah's Witnesses, represented by Hayden Covington, which has occasionally litigated establishment questions.

9. Pennsylvania—School Bus Law (Case No. 2)
Worrell v. Matters, et al.

Plaintiff brough this taxpayer's suit to enjoin the defendants, members of the Rose Tree Union School District (in the Philadelphia suburban area), from providing funds for the transportation of nonpublic school students over public school bus routes pursuant to the 1965 statute also challenged in the *Rhoades* case described above. Plaintiff alleges that the statute is unconstitutional under the separation provisions of the United States and State Constitutions. He also asserts that the statute is unconstitutional on the grounds of vagueness.

This case was started September 5, 1965 in the Court of Common Pleas, Delaware County, Pa. An amended complaint was filed on September 23, 1965. The State and a group of Catholic parents were allowed to intervene as defendants. All defendants filed answers admitting the allegations of fact and asserting that only legal issues were raised. The petition of the Attorney General of Pennsylvania for certiorari to the State Supreme Court, in which the plaintiff joined, was granted and the case was argued in the Supreme Court on April 27, together with the *Rhoades* case, above. However, the plaintiffs in the *Eininger* case below have moved to intervene and have petitioned the Court to withhold decision on both *Rhoades* and *Worrell,* pending a trial of the facts in the *Eininger* case.

Attorney for Plaintiff: William P. Thorn,
150 Allendale Road, King of Prussia, Pa.

Attorney for Defendants: George W. Thompson,
306 So. 69th Street, Upper Darby, Pa.

Attorney for State of Pennsylvania: Attorney General
Walter E. Allesandroni, State Capitol, Harrisburg, Pa.

Attorney for Intervenor-Defendant Parents: Harry Gibbons,
Media, Pa.

Sponsors: American Civil Liberties Union; American
Jewish Congress.

Source: Litigation Docket of Pending Cases Affecting Freedom of Religion and Separation of Church and State, No. 3, June 30, 1966, p. 11, Commission on Law and Social Action American Jewish Congress.

The accommodationist bar is less differentiated and visible. Its central clearing house is the Legal Department of the USCC, and its most distinguished members are William Ball, of Harrisburg, Pennsylvania, and Porter R. Chandler, a partner in the Wall Street firm of Davis, Polk, and Chairman of the Board of Higher Education of the City of

New York. Chandler participated in the *Everson* case, and he and Ball have an interesting way of turning up in important church-state legal battles. As we have noted, Citizens for Educational Freedom is geared mainly to legislative and administrative lobbying and electioneering, but does submit *amicus curiae* briefs from time to time. It did so, for instance, in the Prince Edwards County school case.[17] Here the Commonwealth of Virginia, as part of its resistance to desegregation in public education, was providing tuition grants to students attending private schools. CEF defended the constitutional propriety of tuition grants in general, but objected to the particular Virginia scheme because the grants could only be used at non-sectarian schools.

Obviously the various separationist "legal shops" do not all work in the same way. There are important differences of style and tactics in the way they approach the courts and attempt to influence the shape of constitutional rules. The USCC does not litigate at all, but confines itself to rendering research service, giving advice and arranging for accommodationist intervenors in important cases. Its advice is of a very high quality, and in case after case where the interests of Catholics are involved the USCC, through its legal chief, William Considine, is on hand to smooth out details and furnish arguments. The aggressive AJCongress, by contrast, seeks central control and management of cases from their very beginnings. The Congress initiates cases, and is reluctant to become involved in any litigation after the trial stage. Its director, Will Maslow, has pointed out that his organization seeks to influence the development of law by bringing cases, by offering advice to others engaged in litigation, by issuing statements and research reports, and by submitting *amicus curiae* briefs. But the principal reliance is on bringing cases, and here Maslow feels the record made in the trial court is critical. The AJCongress is usually seeking Supreme Court review, and it feels its chances of getting the right questions before the Court are increased if it can create the record.[18] The ACLU takes a similar line. AU's use of litigation for its local impact value has already been mentioned.

The separationist groups are naturally on the attack in the courts. Characteristically, they want current programs stopped, and they are fairly confident constitutional law will go their way. The accommodationist groups are usually concerned to defend some victory they have won in a legislature or administrative agency. They are less confident that courts are going their way and they have little desire to initiate tests.

It is still possible, of course, for a church-state "freelancer" to begin a case and carry it up to the Supreme Court or the high court of a state. But it is very expensive, and it is likely that even the hardiest self-starter will take advantage of the support and counsel proffered by interest groups. The struggle over the constitutional law of church and state has been best described by its pre-eminent practitioner, Leo Pfeffer—he calls it an "associational jurisprudence."

The Dilemma of "Standing"

One final complication of the constitutional arena must be mentioned: this is the legal problem of standing to sue. Far from being a dry technical matter, the question of standing involves the fundamental and fascinating issue of the proper role of interest groups in the making of constitutional law.

The American legal system is based on highly individualistic assumptions. Our courts adjudicate "live" controversies between aggrieved individuals or corporations as legal persons; they do not answer abstract questions. It is not enough for an interest-group lawyer to say "here is a constitutional wrong which should be righted"; individual plaintiffs must present themselves who are personally injured by the challenged practice. This sounds easy, but in the church-state area it presents serious practical problems. Generally speaking, groups that seek to employ the judicial process to attain their ends do so in one of three ways: first, if the offending governmental action commands or forbids something, the group can arrange to have it defied and raise the desired constitutional point in defense; second, if the group supports a governmental action, it can cooperate with public officials for its vigorous prosecution or defense if under challenge (this course is often followed by accommodationists); and third, if the action is offensive, government officials can be sued to cease and desist. Only the third course is open to separationist groups seeking to challenge governmental expenditures which they believe offend against the establishment clause. In these cases there is no governmental command to disobey and the group's only recourse is to initiate civil action to have the expenditure enjoined.

Yet the separationist group itself has no standing in court to raise objections. The only way of "getting at" governmental expenditures is through a highly suspect form of action—the taxpayer's suit. Such suits are conventionally justified by the argument that the plaintiff's substance is diminished by taxation and he should be able to object if

public money, even a minuscule part of it, is disbursed in an unconstitutional fashion. Unfortunately for separationist legal strategists, the
federal courts will not entertain taxpayer suits challenging expenditures of the Federal Government. The controlling precedent in this matter is *Frothingham v. Mellon,* decided by the Supreme Court in 1923.[19]
A majority held that the interest of a federal taxpayer in an outlay of
the national government was so tiny that it could not be the basis of
legal action. To allow such challenges would be, in effect, to allow
citizens to raise legal questions *pro bono publico,* and not because they
themselves were specifically injured. Speaking for the Court, Justice
Sutherland concluded that:

> The functions of government under our system are apportioned. . . .
> We have no power per se to review and annul acts of Congress
> on the ground that they are unconstitutional. That question may be
> considered only when the justification for some direct injury suffered
> or threatened, presenting a justifiable issue, is made to rest upon
> such an act. . . .[20]

In the states the situation is somewhat easier. Most allow some state
taxpayer actions against state expenditures (only New Mexico and
New York specifically forbid them), and New York City permits them
under its Charter.[21] Furthermore, the Supreme Court has usually been
willing to entertain taxpayer suits against state expenditures coming
from state courts. Thus separationist lawyers find themselves in the
anomalous position of being able to raise First Amendment questions
in state courts concerning state monies with at least the hope of future
Supreme Court consideration, but have no way of challenging what is
done by the Federal Government. In the school prayer cases the problem of standing was lessened because the plaintiffs had children in
school who were directly affected by the religious exercises. It was not
necessary to rely on a taxpayer claim alone. But when it is solely a
question of public money, the taxpayer action, at present at least, is the
only available method.

This sometimes results in practices on the part of separationist groups
which an ill-tempered commentator might describe as devious. Plaintiffs are sought on the basis of their eligibility as taxpayers of particular jurisdictions and are persuaded to lend their names to litigation which
is in fact conceived and prosecuted by the group. Oblique attacks are
often directed against federal programs in local courts based on small
contributions of state money incidental to the expenditure of unchal-

lengeable federal funds. And even when the issue is one which makes it possible to achieve standing on some basis other than taxpayer status, say a school prayer case, this may depend upon an impermanent status. If the child of the parent who challenges a religious exercise in school should graduate while the litigation is making its way up the appelate ladder, the courts may declare the case moot and the whole thing will have to be begun again with new parents or abandoned. Separationist legal strategists live a continuing nightmare of standing problems. Many cases, despite all efforts, are dismissed and have to be written off as a cost of doing separationist business. Much attention is devoted to the prospects of reversing *Frothingham,* and a compelling argument is made that a truly constitutional system should not tolerate the existence of serious constitutional questions which cannot be brought before the courts. Unless challenges are possible, it is said, government officials will be able to spend the public money according to their own whims, with no regard for fundamental law.

The accommodationists, predictably, tend to support the standing rules which make it difficult for separationists to get into court, and decry opening the courts to organizational busybodies. In 1965, after the passage of the Elementary and Secondary Education Act (ESEA), separationist Senator Sam Ervin (D., N.C.), introduced a bill to provide statutory exemption from standing rules and allow all citizens to challenge specified federal statutes, including the ESEA, on First Amendment grounds. In the words of its sponsor it was

> designed to remove any of the existing doubt as to the power of taxpayers, citizens and institutions to obtain judicial review of the validity of Federal grants and loans under the provisions relating to religion in the first amendment.[21]

Extensive hearings were held on Ervin's bill during the spring of 1966, and in instance after instance the witnesses took strict or permissive positions on standing in accordance with their general positions on the proper limits of government cooperation with religion.[23]

At this writing a case is pending before the Supreme Court which asks for re-examination of *Frothingham* in light of the special problems of standing encountered in the church-state area. The genesis of this litigation will be traced in the next chapter. If a majority of the Justices should choose to allow federal taxpayers to raise "establishment questions," the way will be opened for new church-state law-making. Separationist groups have the questions, and if the opportunity is presented they will ask them in rapid fire.*

THE NATIONAL LEGISLATIVE–ADMINISTRATIVE ARENA

Many of us have an image of the lobbyist which is highly colored by the work of political cartoonists. He is traditionally caricatured as a fat cigar-chomping "pressure boy," who seeks to lure legislators and bureaucrats from the paths of virtue and the "public interest" with strong meats, strong waters, the temptations of Eve, or just plain cash. This is regrettable on two counts: first, it oversimplifies the complex process by which interest groups seek to communicate directly with public policy-makers; second, it obscures the essential legitimacy of close relationships between the rulers and spokesmen for the ruled.

Reflection on the notion of "the public interest" quickly reveals its emptiness. It is easy to agree that health and peace are interests which everyone shares, but as soon as a specific proposal is made to improve health services or promote peace, the community splits. Some will favor the proposal, others will not; some will see it as helping their sort of people, others will resent what they see as discrimination or an attempt to reward the unworthy. A plan for improving airports has little appeal to those who stay at home, and a powerful case can be made that one should speak not of the public interest, but of the demands of numerous "publics." The lobbyist is by definition a special pleader, but the sum of all special pleadings is, unless we wish to trust in treacherous notions of natural law or general will, all the "public interest" we have.

Groups seek to lobby in a variety of ways, and a large scholarly literature has grown up on the subject.[24] The following generalizations are intended to convey the conventional wisdom of political scientists concerning Washington lobbying.

First, lobbying is not exclusively a legislative phenomenon. In Washington, and indeed at all levels of government, the agencies charged with administering the law perform highly creative interpretive roles. To apply the general rule to the facts at hand is to take part in making law. When the President signs an engrossed bill this does not end the political struggle, but merely shifts its setting somewhat. Many of the groups that favored or opposed its passage in Congress will follow it carefully as it is given life by an executive or regulatory agency, at-

*The Court did so by a vote of 8-1 on June 10, 1968.

tempting to protect the victories won on the Hill or reverse legislative defeats. The most carefully wrought legislative adjustments, as we shall see, can easily be undone by the decision or indecision of an administrator as to what a section of an act means. In most cases the "congressional intent" was contradictory or purposefully ill-defined. The administrator must himself decide "who gets the lemons," or find some way of dodging the matter. Alternatively, when a group is aggrieved by the way in which an agency is administering a law, it may "appeal" to Congress to amend the statute, restate its intent, or at least make it a bit more difficult for the bureaucrats to behave as they are. Issues move from Congress to administrative agencies and back again in a dialectical process of statement, definition, restatement and redefinition. This continuing politics includes groups operating both downtown and on Capitol Hill, often attempting to use one against the other.

Second, while there are certainly occasional resorts to bribery, and while some lobbyists seem compulsively lavish in their hospitality, there is little of political value in Washington which is simply for sale. Interest group representatives proceed more subtly and much more systematically. They may achieve privileged access by providing research or bill-drafting services for friendly senators and representatives who are understaffed. Group leaders can attempt to persuade legislators by instituting letter-writing campaigns, or attempt to impress administrators by reminding them of the group's friends in Congress. Contributions to campaigns and promises to employ a group's internal channels of communication to the benefit of a particular candidate are also coins of exchange. Complicated log-rolling and alliance-formation goes on continually. Groups with a serious interest in affecting the legislative process are careful to build close, continuing relations with legislative assistants and committee employees—the nonelected legislative actors. Group leaders may also give testimony before congressional committees. Although no one's position is changed by what happens during these repetitive rituals, groups can earn credit with a legislator simply by appearing and swelling the ranks of those recorded as supporting his bill. In all of this—both legislative and administrative lobbying— perhaps the most important element is reliable intelligence. The lobbyist must know what is happening if he is to reach key people before options are foreclosed. The group representative's most important resource is regular communication with key people in his area of policy concern.

Of course the relationship between groups and policy-makers is reciprocal. It is not only that the group representatives need the decision-makers; the decision-makers often have need of the groups. We have noted how a legislator may attempt to marshal group support behind a bill during the course of hearings, and the importance to him of good relations with numerically powerful groups is obvious. The administrator also has need of group support. If powerful social formations immediately affected by his programs are unreconciled or actively opposed to his efforts they can make his task—whether he is setting air-safety standards or aiding education—considerably more difficult. Indeed, strong interest groups may even destroy a program unless the administrator can count on support from other powerful quarters such as the White House. But if the administrator has managed to establish good relations with a group or groups that care deeply about what he is doing, they can be a source of considerable advantage and security to him. A friendly group "constituency" can offer protection to the administrator in the appropriations process and in seeking new legislative grants of authority.

Groups and governmental leaders are constantly reaching out to one another. This complicated communications net, which cannot be neatly described or located geographically like the Bureau of Standards or the Supreme Court, is nonetheless an institution of our national government. Some groups participate effectively, some do not. Numbers, money, social status and the skills of leaders are important, but they are not automatic guarantees of success. The only way to find out how well particular groups are doing, is to examine closely particular policy areas.

Washington lobbying by groups concerned with church-state relations reflects the general characteristics of the process just described. An excellent illustration is the group interaction over the Elementary and Secondary Education Act of 1965. This program embodied a delicate compromise of the non-public-school issue on which President Kennedy's aid to education proposals had foundered in 1961 and 1962. This compromise has become the subject of continuing lobbying which reaches remarkable complexity.

In 1962 Hugh Douglas Price wrote of the Kennedy education battles that

> There were at least three discernible levels of disagreement. On the first level there were low-temperature disputes over detailed matters of program administration, state allocation formulas, and so forth

that could be adjusted by normal bureaucratic and interest group bargaining. Such disputes would exist even if there were a clear national consensus in favor of federal aid.

At an intermediate level was the more basic split over the desirability of such a program, typified by the opposing views of the National Education Association and the U.S. Chamber of Commerce. This sort of conflict can still be handled, although it becomes difficult if the issues are framed in symbolic terms ("federal aid" versus "federal control").

At a third level, such high-temperature issues as segregation and the role of parochial schools are generally beyond the ability of Congress to handle. Next to being shot up by Puerto Rican nationalists (as happened in 1954), there are few less appealing prospects, especially for the House, than a floor fight combining race, religion, and control of the schools.[25]

The Catholic Conference, the National Education Association, and the separationist groups were still at loggerheads when, in January 1965, Lyndon Johnson confronted the new 89th Congress and sent his aid to education package to the Hill. The Johnson formula for breaking the church-state aspect of the deadlock on federal aid to education was twofold: first, his proposals were aimed at a special category of children, the poor and educationally disadvantaged; second, students in non-public-schools would be able to participate in certain of the compensatory programs to be established.

These programs were of three sorts. First, there was a provision for "shared time" whereby non-public-school students might take certain courses in a public school while spending the rest of the day in a parochial setting; in addition, there was provision for certain "shared services" which could be provided *in non-public schools* (Title I). Second, funds were to be provided for library books which would be available to all the children of the community, including those in non-public schools, but would be publicly owned (Title II). Third, provision was made for the creation of "supplementary educational centers" offering expensive "extras" such as exhibitions of the graphic and performing arts. These centers would be publicly operated, but would remain separate from the regular public schools and available for use by students from nonpublic institutions (Title III). In short, Johnson's package represented a modified individual-benefit approach as opposed to Kennedy's strict separationism.

The Administration's opening political gambit was a meeting between Commissioner of Education Francis C. Keppel and representa-

tives from two key groups—the National Catholic Welfare Conference
(as it was then) and the National Education Association. It was
pointed out to the two groups that Congress, with its new Democratic
majorities, was ready to pass an education bill, and if the groups
wished to preserve their bargaining positions they had better áccept the
essentials of the Administration's proposals.[26] This message, backed by
Johnson's 61 percent of the popular vote and the 58 nonsouthern fresh-
men Democrats in the House of Representatives, got through. The
NCWC and the NEA approached the Johnson proposals prepared for
limited bargaining and anxious to find a mutually satisfactory
adjustment.

The second phase in the Administration's campaign involved a wider
range of groups. Assistant Secretary of Health, Education and Welfare
Wilbur Cohen and Commissioner Keppel communicated through their
staffs with the separationist Consortium which had been organized
around Dean Kelley of the National Council of Churches, and with
the individual organizations on both sides of the question. The initial
understanding worked out with the NCWC and the NEA was used
as an example of "responsibility" in this effort to lever other groups
into line. The NEA leadership made it clear to separationist groups
such as the ACLU and the NCC, which had been its allies on the
church-state question in previous aid-to-education battles, that it was
prepared to accept a compromise along the line suggested by the Administration. As one separationist leader put it, "NEA went dead in
the water." Douglass Cater, a Special Assistant to the President and
the White House aide with particular responsibility for the education
program, was visited by the leaders of separationist groups including
the ACLU, the AJCommittee and the NCC. Cater told them that it
was no part of the President's purpose to aid church-related schools.
and that the bill should be viewed in the context of the newly declared War on Poverty.[27]

This Cohen-Keppel-Cater effort to extend the NCWC–NEA understanding through the entire spectrum of church-state interest groups
was only partially successful. The National Council of Churches, with
considerable trepidation, agreed to go along with the individual-benefit
approach if the limited nature of the "special services" to be available
in non-public-schools were clearly spelled out. The Baptist Joint Committee on Public Affairs also took this position. But the AJCongress,
the ACLU and AU continued to oppose any publicly financed services
in non-public-schools. Citizens for Educational Freedom, interestingly,

was also hostile to the Johnson bill because it did not go far enough in aiding non-public-school students and seemed to relegate them to "second-class citizenship." Just as the NCC was unable to move the strict separationist groups to a more flexible position, so the NCWC was unable to bring along CEF.

During this initial congressional phase, much important bargaining took place directly between the moderate separationists, led by the NCC, and the moderate accommodationists, the NCWC and its friends in Congress. The Administration's managers were eager to placate both sides without sacrificing any essential element of the proposals, and without accepting anything they regarded as administratively unworkable. The bill, which finally passed Congress and was signed by the President on April 11 (less than three months after the original proposals went up), was hammered out within the General Education Subcommittee of the House Education and Labor Committee.[28] Three major church-state points were in dispute; in ascending order of troublesomeness these involved (1) the participation of parochial school officials in managing the Title-III supplementary centers, (2) whether the library books provided for in Title II could be given directly to private schools or whether they should be controlled by a public authority and made available under some loan system to children in non-public-schools, and (3) the circumstances under which public school teachers might go into private schools under the "shared services" provision of Title I.

The first two issues were resolved more or less to the satisfaction of the separationists. It was made clear in the subcommittee revision of the bill that the Title III centers would be separate from the regular public schools, but under the control of local public school boards. In the matter of library books, it was provided that ownership should be public and that there should be no direct grants to private schools (exactly how the use of the books was to be managed was left unclear, and has continued to cause trouble). On the issue of what shared services might be provided in private schools, however, there was a conflict between the separationist and accommodationist bargainers which proved exceedingly difficult to adjust—so difficult that a resort to ambiguity was necessary in order that the bill pass on for full committee action and then to the floor. A distinction was developed between "special" educational services, which might (if no alternative means were available) be rendered on private school premises, and "general" educational services, which non-public-school students would have to go into a public school to obtain. The problem then became what was "special." The subcommittee avoided a definition, but this omission was ruthlessly exposed by enemies of the bill when it reached the floor of the House. The following colloquy is typical of the debate. Representative Charles Goodell (R., N.Y.), who opposed the bill as a whole, is making mischief; Representative Hugh Carey (D., N.Y.), the staunchest supporter of the private school cause within the subcommittee, is attempting to create a legislative history to justify the widest possible range of services in church-related schools; Representative Carl Perkins (D., Ky.), the Chairman of the subcommittee, and a man inclined to take the separationists seriously, is attempting to preserve a necessary degree of ambiguity and keep a delicate political balance from tipping.

> Mr. Goodell: What instruction would be given in private schools? Would that include the services of a music teacher?
> Mr. Carey: I would say a music teacher, yes, where that would be a definite need, but that would be provided for in the local educational agency.
> Mr. Goodell: Does it include a speech therapist?
> Mr. Carey: I should think so, but I am not making the judgment for the local public educational agencies.
> Mr. Goodell: Would it include a teacher of remedial reading?
> Mr. Carey: I should think remedial reading would be a subject that could be included.
> Mr. Goodell: So the gentleman from New York is of the opinion that public school teachers may teach on private school premises; is that right?
> Mr. Carey: I must answer the question with a question. Who else would provide the service if he did not?
> Mr. Goodell: Then the gentleman's answer is yes. I would like to ask the gentleman from Kentucky if that is his answer, just as a matter of getting the legislative history.
> Mr. Perkins: The gentleman has answered the question very clearly.
> Mr. Goodell: Then the answer is yes?
> Mr. Perkins: My answer is no as to providing any teaching services to a private institution. The key here is the extension of special educational services to deprived children under public auspices and arranged for, supervised, and controlled by public authority.
> Mr. Goodell: All right, then, we have a nice, clear legislative history to proceed with. Nobody knows what this bill is going to do.
> Mr. Perkins: There are special services to which I would say "yes," but generally "no."[29]

A possible disaster was averted at this point by the introduction of new, "clarifying" language by Representative Frank Thompson (D., N.J.). The formula was drafted by Administrative representatives, and intended to serve as the compromise legislative history on the point— a position to which all supporters of the bill could repair.

> Mr. Thompson: Services and arrangements provided for nonpublic school students in nonpublic schools must be special as distinguished from general educational assistance. The decision about the best arrangement for providing special educational assistance under Title I is left to the public education agency of the school district, under the Constitution and laws of the State. Thus, public school boards could make available the services of such special personnel as guidance counsellors, speech therapists, remedial reading specialists, school social workers who would reach the nonpublic schoolchildren in the public schools or through public services in the nonpublic buildings, or through mobile services, or through ETV, or through community centers, etc. But these special services would not be part of the regular instructional program of the nonpublic schools and the nonpublic schools could not get general classroom teachers in history, English, mathematics and social studies.[30]

After President Johnson's numerous pens had done their work, the focus of the struggle shifted downtown to the Office of Education. In administering a grant program such as the ESEA, a set of guidelines are issued by the responsible federal agency to tell their prospective claimants how the program is to work. These guidelines are of crucial importance for the interest groups involved. These rules, not the text of the Act, exactly determine "who gets what—when, where and how." The first draft of the Office of Education guidelines became available in the late summer of 1965, and the moderate separationists who had supported the Act as an individual-benefit compromise were horrified. As two of them put it later,

> imagine the surprise of the church-state specialists, then, when they obtained copies of the first draft of the administrative regulations . . . and discovered that many of the central terms of the church-state settlement were completely missing from the draft regulations!
> Since most local administrators would probably never see the Act itself, let alone read the committee reports of the record of the legislative debates, their entire impression of the law would be gained from the administrative regulations of the U.S. Office of Education and the State regulations based upon them. If these regulations were to omit the crucial church-state settlement worked out in Congress, very little reliable guidance would be available for them in developing their state and local programs under the Act in conformity to that settlement.[31]

Immediate separationist representations were made to Commissioner Keppel and to John Gardner, the new Secretary of Health, Education and Welfare. In response to charges of faithlessness to the intent of Congress, the Office of Education produced a revised set of guidelines which finally appeared in the *Federal Register* of September 15. This revised version made a bow to the Thompson formula on special services in private schools, but it was obvious that an alternative interpretation of the legislative history was being urged by the NCWC and that the Office of Education draftsmen were walking a fine line. The separationists regarded the revised guidelines as an improvement over the first draft, but still as an inadequate reflection of what had been "settled" in Congress.

The implementation of the Act through the first year of its life confirmed separationist fears, and opened the moderates to the "we told you so's" of the strict separationists who had refused to have anything to do with the compromise. The guidelines, it was charged, were not being observed by the states, and the separationists claimed that the Office of Education was not fulfilling its enforcement responsibilities. The non-public-schools were getting benefits which the separationists regarded as beyond anything contemplated by Congress, and certainly beyond anything to which they had agreed. With the Act due to come up for renewal and amendment in the spring of 1966, and the Administration preparing to ask for a four-year extension, Dean Kelley convened the Consortium, canvassed other separationist leaders, and prepared to go back to Congress.

The separationists pointed to two major administrative abuses: (1) public school teachers were being sent into private schools under Title I to render general services not comprehended by the Thompson formula, and (2) library books purchased under Title II were not being publicly controlled for the use of the entire community but were simply being given to schools, including private schools, with only a fiction of public ownership maintained. Reports detailing these practices were prepared by the Commission on Religious Liberty of the National Council of Churches and circulated widely among separationists. On April 8, 1966, a group from the separationist Consortium, headed by Kelley, met with the new Commissioner of Education, Harold Howe II. Included in the group were Emanuel Carlson, of the Baptist Joint Committee on Public Affairs, and H. Benjamin Sissel, Secretary for National Affairs of the United Presbyterian Churches in the U.S.A. The meeting was something less than a success. Kelley briefly sketched the separationist case, reminded Commissioner Howe that the separationists had the promise of the Chairman of the General Education Subcommittee (Representative Perkins) that the intent of Congress would be carried out, and pointedly asked what the Commissioner intended to do. Howe then asked that the objections be specified in detail to his aides. Kelley replied that those aides had had the information for months, that he had spent many hours going over it with them, and that there seemed little purpose in doing it all again. The Commissioner replied that he would give their objections serious consideration, but that he was under many pressures. The meeting broke up with Carlson remarking that unless the Office of Education found a way of maintaining "minimal church-state standards" he would have to confess to his constituents that he had misadvised them as to the workability and acceptability of the ESEA.

Kelley had already drafted an article for *The Christian Century* accusing the Office of Education of ignoring the church-state settlement which the Johnson Administration had undertaken to support and which had cleared the way for the passage of the Act. After the Howe meeting, a carbon of this piece was sent to Douglass Cater, and Cater set up a hurried meeting at the White House with Kelley. Cater expressed his dismay at the article, and asked for time to iron out administrative difficulties. He sent Kelley on to Wilbur Cohen, by then Under Secretary of HEW, who promised that the 1966 Education Act amendments, then in preparation, would clarify the original settlement and adequately provide for the correction of what the separationists regarded as abuses. Specifically, Cohen promised to insert a provision for financing community repositories for books purchased under Title II, and agreed to the need for clearer definition of the sorts of special services which could be provided on private school premises. As a result of these conversations, Kelley moderated both the *Christian Century* article (which appeared on May 11) and the testimony which he later delivered during the Senate hearings on the amendments.

The outcome of the second legislative round of the ESEA battle can only be regarded as a standoff. Cohen had claimed to be confident that the NCWC and Representative Hugh Carey would go along with certain concessions to the separationists, but this did not prove the case. The provision for Title II book repositories was gutted in subcommittee at Carey's behest. The new language concerning "special services" in the full House Education and Labor Committee report on the amendments so alarmed accommodationists, and gave rise to such pressure from the NCWC, that the Committee resorted to the bizarre expedient of issuing a "Part 2" to its report, which churned new mud into the waters. The original report had specified that the "special services" which could be performed on private school premises were "remedial," and that

> "remedial services" are those which assist children in *basic* language and computation skills such as remedial reading and remedial arithmetic. "Remedial" as it relates to the programs permitted on non-public property does *not* include projects or programs which add to or *supplant the regular private school curriculum.* (Emphasis in original.)[32]

The hurriedly prepared Part 2 stated that nothing in Part I should be read as altering anything in the previous legislative history, and it quoted a critical statement from the National Advisory Council on the Education of Disadvantaged Children to the effect that private school children were *not* participating in ESEA programs to the extent contemplated by Congress.[33] The Committee associated itself with this sentiment, and stressed the need of cooperation between public and private educators. From the point of view of the separationists, this substantially nullified the force of the report as a whole.

Thus the conflict proceeds. The groups continue to work in the Office of Education and on the congressional committees. The ESEA is being renewed for one-year periods and the lobbying concerning it is year-round. The professionals who make up the church-state "attentive public" realize that the 1965 law is only a beginning. They are poised to struggle over the implications of every substantive change or administrative nuance which might affect the relationship between public and non-public-schools. The intractable positions of the Kennedy years have been moderated somewhat, but on the day this was written the President of the Methodist Council of Bishops warned his denominational convention in sweeping terms against what he called the "strongest pressure" being exerted by the Roman Catholic Church to secure public support for its parochial schools.[34]

THE STATE-AND-LOCAL ARENA

The third arena of conflict encompasses non-judicial church-state encounters at the state and local levels. Here are waged those intimate little community wars over religious practices in particular schools; here are the disputes over religious services and artifacts in public parks; here are the controversies over contraceptive services and hospital practices. State legislatures, mayors, school boards and municipal councils are the foci of struggle, and a frequent result is disruption in the relations between local religious groups. The major church-state groups have local branches and enter state and local struggles from time to time. Characteristically, however, the principal actors are most often local churches, ministerial associations, fraternal organizations and professional groups. These are church-state amateurs, and their principal weapon is propaganda—propaganda which all too often crosses the line of defamation. These state and local disruptions may be triggered by some governmental innovation (moving the high school baccalaureate to a Protestant church), or by demographic changes which bring new minorities into previously homogeneous areas. Characteristically these conflicts heat rapidly until a test of political forces has settled the particular point at issue. Political interaction usually ceases at once, but the lingering bitterness which can be engendered when a community is split along confessional lines is surprising in what we are pleased to think of as an increasingly tolerant and urbane society.

It is precisely because of the amateur and intermittent character of church-state conflicts at the state and local levels that they deserve separate treatment. In the constitutional and national legislative-administrative arenas the struggles are usually managed by professionals—by interest-group tacticians who are more or less full-time church-state "hands." This is necessary for carrying forward complicated campaigns of litigation, and for maintaining the complex communication networks on which effective lobbying in Washington depends. In the states and localities, church-state conflicts are much less structured, and the techniques of political action differ from those of the first two arenas. The emphasis is not on long-range planning and carefully established access to key decision-makers, but rather on rapid marshaling of community sentiment and support for one highly moralized battle—to stop a particular bill in a state legislature, or to force a school board to refrain from doing something. Typically, ad hoc group coalitions develop quickly, activity rises to a climax, some decision is taken and the coalitions dissolve—leaving more or less serious community relations wounds. The amateurs return to their separate concerns, national groups which intervened close their files and church-state activity ceases until another issue blows up.

An excellent example of the way in which church-state issues arise at the local level is the battle in New York City during 1956 and 1957 over the so-called "Lincoln Square" urban renewal project.

When a plan to redevelop the dilapidated area around Lincoln Square (Broadway and 61st Street on Manhattan's West Side) was announced in April 1955, the *New York Times* greeted it with enthusiasm. It would "replace a generally dreary, dismal neighborhood with no future in the main except certain decline,"[35] with modern, well-planned, socially useful buildings. Nor was the *Times* alone in its approval. Almost immediately, potential developers, city-planning groups and influential individuals offered support. John D. Rockefeller III began to mobilize potential patrons behind the idea of a performing arts complex, and to boost the project as a whole.

The scheme, which eventually included an irregularly shaped area between 60th and 69th Streets, was undertaken under Title I of the Federal Housing Act of 1949. This provided that "a city or other local public agency may acquire slum sites and make them available for redevelopment by private capital subject to plans approved by the municipality and the Federal Government."[36] In other words, the city condemned the land and buildings, and the Federal Government paid the lion's share of the costs of compensating the owners and clearing the land. Once the land was cleared by this procedure it was sold at attractive prices (far below the cost of acquisition and clearance) to private developers.

Church-state trouble arose over Lincoln Square when it was announced that Fordham University (a Jesuit institution) would participate as a developer. On April 18, the *Times* noted that criticism of aid to a religious institution was being voiced, but quoted a spokesman for Fordham who "emphasized the university is non-sectarian."[37] The major attack on the project came from a tenants' group (mostly small businessmen) protesting inadequate provision for relocation of those to be displaced by the clearance. This ad hoc group, led by a New York attorney named Harris Present, quickly played up the church-state issue in order to gain allies. A number of Protestant ministers entered the fray, demanding the cancellation of the project if Fordham were included. The national headquarters of Americans United sent in speakers and funds to prevent a "land grab" by a sectarian institution at public expense. Rallies were held, sermons were preached, and advertisements stating the tenants' case and the separationists' case appeared in the press.

The premium was on rapid mobilization of the broadest antirenewal coalition in the shortest possible time. Robert Moses, the wily and determined survivor of a score of such protest efforts, was masterminding the project. Its opponents knew they would be beaten unless they could slow the pace which Moses was setting, and keep the project from gaining momentum. Twice they forced postponements of the crucial decision by the City Board of Estimate (the most important branch of the municipal legislature), and charges and counter-charges were exchanged for over a year. Finally, however, on November 26, 1957, (with the mayoral election safely out of the way), the Board voted approval of the project and Mayor Wagner gave his blessing and promises that adequate provision would be made for relocation.[38] The church-state issue was brushed aside.

Present then attempted to move into the constitutional arena with a case testing the permissibility of participation by a religious institution in a Title I program. Although AU contributed some funds to this effort, other professional separationist groups decided that the First Amendment argument was not strong enough to justify costs and risk creating unfortunate precedents. They saw Fordham's participation as a violation, but not a clear enough case to promise a judicial victory. The doubters were right. The attempt to "constitutionalize" failed in the lower courts. AU pulled out, and the buildings (including Fordham's) went up. As a battle at the local level Lincoln Square was bitter but limited in duration. As an issue in the constitutional arena it failed to attract much professional support and soon foundered.

CHAPTER FOUR

THE CASE
OF NEW YORK

Over the past few years New York has been caught up in a deepening church-state controversy which (1) illustrates the dynamics of three arenas of conflict, (2) reflects almost the full spectrum of church-state issues which vex America today, and (3) clearly reveals the disruptive potential of such issues. What is happening in New York is more bruising and more widely publicized than what is happening elsewhere, but the elements of this continuing conflict are by no means unique.

New York (and especially New York City) has a long history of church-state tension. Since World War II, there have been flare-ups over, among other things, religiously inspired censorship, birth-control programs, released-time programs, and participation of religious institutions in urban renewal programs. Until the mid-1960's, however, these ructions were occasional and discrete. As is characteristic of conflicts in the state-and-local arena, they blew up quickly, caused a little blood to be spilt and were over quickly. Now the New York struggle has become permanent and very costly. There appear to be three causes of this change: Governor Rockefeller, the Elementary and Secondary Education Act of 1965 and the effort in 1967 to revise the state's constitution.

ROCKEFELLER AND PRIVATE EDUCATION

Nelson Rockefeller desires to make a record as a Governor who substantially improved education in his state. He is also faced with a situation in which about 39 percent of the state's elementary school students, 12 percent of its secondary school students and a substantial portion of those pursuing higher education are enrolled in non-public-schools. As a matter of morals and of electoral politics (a happy conjunction), he has committed his administration to doing something for all students, including nonpublic ones.

A start was made at the college level in 1961, when Rockefeller proposed an amendment to the New York Constitution which would have allowed the state to issue bonds and make loans for facilities construction at private colleges and universities whether church-related or not. At the time the Governor took his decision it must have seemed a modest step. Separationists were supposed to feel less strongly about aid to institutions of higher education than about aid to church-related elementary and secondary schools, and, in any case, loans were an "arm's-length" sort of aid. The separationist reaction, however, was sharp, and the proposal became the subject of intense criticism. Local civic and religious groups received help from professional separationist groups in warning the electorate of the perils of the scheme. Four of the five newspapers then published in New York City opposed it, and when the amendment was presented to the voters in the November 1961 election it was soundly defeated.

But the Governor was only beginning. Resorting to a standard technique of frustrated New York chief executives, he had created an "independent authority" which issued bonds and made the loans which the electorate had just denied the state the power to make. And the next year he developed and piloted through the legislature a "scholar incentive program" which provided grants to students in good standing at accredited institutions. This did not require a constitutional amendment and was never put before the voters. The student simply applied for the grant, and if he was registered and breathing, the money was given. This was, of course, little more than a system of indirect subsidy to the institutions. Colleges and universities were able to raise tuition by the amount of the scholar-incentive payment and rake in the new money without actually charging the students. The students became conduits for channeling funds to church-related schools which it might have been illegal to aid directly (raising problems under both the state and federal constitutions).[1] Separationists blustered and charged sham, but the State of New York does not allow taxpayer suits against itself, and there was no way in which the program could be tested.*

---

*As was mentioned in Chapter III, New York City does allow such actions. This distinction will become important later in this case study.

Then in 1965, the Governor secured the passage of a bill providing for state grants to school districts for the purchase of textbooks which were to be "loaned" to students in grades 7 through 12 in non-public-schools.[2] Separationist elements within the state made a concerted effort to block the bill. This time, they had a great deal of help from the professional separationist groups who were coming to look upon New York as a kind of church-state proving ground for the nation. Beaten in the Legislature where they had been caught off balance, the separationist opposition drew together and gained strength after the passage of the bill. The new law was not to take effect until September 1, 1966, and in the meantime the Governor was attempting to increase the maximum amount allowable per child from $10.00 to $25.00 for the first year's operations. This sent the matter back to the Legislature in the 1966 session, where the amendment met stiff opposition from liberal New York City Democrats who attacked church-school aid as subversion of the public school system. On May 20, 1966, a news conference was held at the headquarters of the AJCongress. Present were representatives of the New York Civil Liberties Union (the state affiliate of the ACLU), the Anti-Defamation League, the Citizens Committee for the Children of New York, the Public Education Association, the United Parents Association, the Protestant Council of the City of New York and, interestingly enough, the Urban League of Greater New York (a Negro rights group). All voiced opposition to the textbook program on church-state grounds.[3] This represented the beginning of a specialized New York City separationist consortium which functioned with considerable effectiveness over the next several months.[4]

The Governor finally compromised on the question of maximum payments, setting these at $15.00 for the first year and $10.00 for each year thereafter. This amendment passed the Legislature, and the separationists began to look for a way of getting into court. The New York Civil Liberties Union assumed the responsibilities for securing a test, but as taxpayers had no standing to sue, the NYCLU director, Aryeh Neier, was faced with the old problem of who could raise the constitutional questions. His ingenious answer was—a local school board. Under the law these bodies were charged with spending the funds and furnishing the books to the non-public-schools. One board was found, the majority of which believed that the textbook program was unconstitutional and which was willing to carry its opposition to the point of suing for an injunction to prevent the state Commissioner of Education from implementing the program. This school board (in the Albany suburb of East Greenbush) was later joined by the school officials from other counties. In both communities, NYCLU activists were instrumental in persuading the boards to take their stands, and in both there was substantial accommodationist opposition which threatened retaliation at the polls in the next school board election. The standing of school boards to challenge state action was by no means clear—school boards are themselves arms of the state—but this was the best the separationist legal strategists could do. A group of Catholic parents of students in the parochial schools of East Green- bush were allowed to intervene in the case on the grounds that they might be directly affected by the result, and it was arranged through the New York Catholic Welfare Conference that Porter Chandler, the dean of accommodationist lawyers, act for them.

The first round went to the separationists when, on August 19, 1966, Justice Paul T. Kane of the State Supreme Court (the trial level in New York) held the textbook program unconstitutional on both state and federal grounds. This ruling spread confusion through many school districts which had already ordered books for their private schools,[5] but many of the state's public educators probably agreed with the editorial board of the *Times* which declared that Judge Kane's de- cision "has hit at the dangerous erosion of the separation of church and state in many current school-aid programs."[6] A spokesman for the publishing firm of Houghton-Mifflin noted that his employees had been working overtime for several weeks to fill New York orders for non- public-schools, and ruefully predicted, "Now they are going to dump it all back in our lap and say 'sorry.' "[7]

Governor Rockefeller, however, quickly moved to rescue the pro- gram. State Attorney-General Louis Lefkowitz, while taking the oppor- tunity to point out that he had advised the Governor the year before that the textbook program raised serious constitutional questions, an- nounced that the state would appeal, and secured a stay of the re- straining order which Judge Kane had issued prohibiting any disbur- sals under the new law. Thus encouraged, the New York City Board of Education announced on September 14 that it was going ahead with purchases and loans to non-public-schools. The Attorney General gave further assurances that books could be given out and that the school districts would be reimbursed by the state under the contested law before the Appellate Division (the intermediate appeals court in New York) reached a decision,[8] and with the risk of loss thus reduced, most school boards in the State followed the City's lead.

Amid separationist charges that the New York City Board of Education was discriminating against public schools by filling orders for non-public-schools first, the program got underway.[9] On New Year's Eve, 1966, the Appellate Division threw out the case on the grounds that the East Greenbush and Roslyn boards lacked standing to sue, and the NYCLU immediately announced that the issue would be carried to the New York Court of Appeals (the state's highest) and to the Supreme Court of the United States if necessary.[10] The Court of Appeals, which handed down its decision on June 1, 1967, reversed the Appellate Division on standing, holding that the East Greenbush board could sue, but then reversed Judge Kane on the merits. The textbook loan scheme was approved by a vote of four of the seven judges despite the strict provision of the New York Constitution barring aid to church-related schools—a provision which, as we shall presently see, was itself to become a matter of violent controversy.[11]

The Governor meanwhile, continued his efforts to get greater amounts of state money working for the benefit of students in non-public-schools. He quietly worked for a removal of the strict constitutional prohibition of aid to church schools, and on March 4, 1967, he announced the appointment of a committee of five educators, chaired by McGeorge Bundy, President of the Ford Foundation, to seek new ways of aiding private institutions of higher learning in the state. The committee, the *Times* reported, "will face the problem of how to provide aid . . . without violating the State Constitution. . . ."[12] Each new Rockefeller move has brought more strident cries from separationists, but the Governor has persevered as the temperature of church-state politics has risen.*

THE ESEA: LEGACY OF CONFLICT

One result of the passage of the Elementary and Secondary Education Act was to extend an on-going church-state conflict from the national legislative-administrative arena to the state-and-local arena. The "settlement" in Congress had been possible only because so much was

---

*The NYCLU carried the case to the United States Supreme Court which held, as previously noted, that the program did not violate the federal First Amendment.

left up to local officials operating under the general USOE guidelines discussed in Chapter III. Many communities became involved in implementation battles. New York City, in the vernacular, had a dilly—that unfolded concurrently with the battle over Rockefeller's textbook loan law. Both Titles I and II presented difficulties, but this discussion will be restricted to the problems posed by Title I.

The ESEA included a formula (based on the number of children from families with incomes below a specified poverty line) for determining how much Title I money went to individual school districts. This left three critical questions to be answered at the community level. First, what specific programs should be initiated? The Act did not dictate these. Certain types of programs were mentioned in the text and suggested by the legislative history, but local authorities were given a great deal of freedom to innovate. Second, in what ways should non-public-school students be involved in these programs? The Act required that local public authorities make some provision for nonpublic students as a condition of receiving federal funds, but again nothing was specified. The Thompson formula sought only to set outer limits to the services which could be rendered in private schools. Third—a particularly difficult question in New York City—how was it to be determined what schools were entitled to participate in Title I programs? The Act did specify that only the educationally disadvantaged could be aided, and not students generally. The Office of Education determined allocations *to* particular school districts, but *within* the districts the educational authorities were left to determine for themselves which schools were "poor."

The Numbers Game

In June of 1965, shortly after the passage of the ESEA, Dr. Bernard Donovan, Superintendent of Schools in New York City, took the initiative in urging the formation of a committee of private school educators to participate with public authorities in planning for the inclusion of nonpublic students in ESEA programs. The result was the Committee of Non-Public-School Officials. Headed by the Very Reverend Eugene J. Molloy, Secretary of the Catholic Schools, Diocese of Brooklyn, this body included representatives of the National Society for Hebrew Day Schools, the Lutheran Day Schools (both Missouri and New York Synods), the Greek Orthodox Day Schools, the Jewish Education Committee of New York, the Episcopal Boarding and Day Schools and the Catholic Schools, Archdiocese of New York. Although formed at the suggestion of a public official to facilitate communication, the Committee soon emerged as the spokesman and bargaining agent of the non-public-schools in the process of implementing ESEA in New York City. Father Molloy proved a tough and skillful fighter, and the Committee's record is impressive. The vast majority of the city's private school students were, of course, in Catholic parochial schools. These have an enrollment of approximately 400,000 (elementary and secondary), and the representatives of other church schools have generally followed Catholic cues.

There was a good deal of quiet maneuvering among public and private schoolmen in the city during late 1965 and early 1966 over plans for implementation of Title I. Then, during the spring and summer of 1966, combat began in earnest when the Board of Education held hearings on its tentative implementation plans. On the question of specific programs, the Board revealed that remedial instruction in regular subjects—especially reading and arithmetic—would be made available in certain private schools. It also became clear that it was precisely these on-the-premises services which interested private school educators, and that they were not at all excited about having their students participate in the public school programs which the Board was proposing. Their position was quite simple—give us our share of the remedial teachers to teach in our schools, and let us forget about moving our students to public schools for music, drama and other frills.[13]

In vain the separationists protested that the intent of Congress, as expressed in the Thompson formula, was that instruction take place on church school premises only in unusual situations where all other alternatives had been explored and found unworkable. In vain they argued that the private schools were obtaining publicly paid teachers for regular subjects which had been dubbed "remedial" but were not the sort of welfare service (speech therapy, instruction for brain-damaged children, etc.) which Congress had conceived of as "special."[14] Father Molloy also kept up the pressure by giving grudging approval of the tentative plans, but promising that if sufficient remedial services were not made available in non-public-schools "the Conmittee of Non-Public-School Officials will be forced to call upon the Congressional Delegation from New York City to take the appropriate action to protect the rights of non-public-school children in the city."[15]

There was also difficulty over the question of which non-public-schools were "poor," and thus entitled to have programs under the Act. For the public schools, the Board of Education's answer was clear:

only facilities physically located in designated low-income areas of the city were eligible. But the private schools often drew their enrollments from wide areas of the city. Although a parochial school was not located in a low-income area, it might have many poor children among its students. Elaborate schemes were discussed for counting the poor children in·private schools, and ratios of remedial instructors to children were negotiated.

It was finally decided that any private school with ten percent or more of its students qualifying for the federal school lunch program would be eligible for on-site remedial programs under the ESEA. This was a considerably more lenient standard than that applied to the public schools which had to be located in low-income neighborhoods in order to be eligible, and thus had enrollments made up almost completely of "poverty children." Also, Superintendent Donovan (as agent for the Board of Education) agreed that the city would supply one remedial teacher for every 100 students for reading and mathematics programs in eligible non-public-schools. This drew immediate fire, as the prevailing ratio in the public schools was one remedial teacher to 230 students. Father Molloy countered that the public school ratio was scandalously low, and that Donovan's proper course was to raise it, not impose it on the private schools. If the public schools wanted low remedial ratios they were free to spend their share of the ESEA money in this way rather than on other enrichment programs.

Through September and October, criticism of the one to 100 private school ratio mounted, with the NYCLU and the United Parents Association (representing the city's public school PTA's) in the vanguard of the separationist attack. On November 8, Superintendent Donovan began what might be described as a classical vacillation. He gave in to separationist demands and reassigned 125 remedial teachers who had been scheduled into private schools. This equalized the ratio at 1 to 230.[16] It also meant the loss of perhaps a half million dollars in services to the non-public-schools, and Molloy's Committee reacted swiftly. A hearing was held on November 14 before the Board of Education, and Father Molloy announced that his constituents could not cooperate in the implementation of the ESEA in New York City unless the cut was restored. He remarked that the move was obviously a "response to UPA (United Parents Association) criticism," and told the Board that he intended

to formally request the New York State Commissioner of Education

[who must approve all local plans under the ESEA] to withhold
approval from these proposals and the United States Office of Education to hold up the funding of the entire New York City Title I
program until it can assure the public and the Congress that the intent of Congress in behalf of non-public school children has been
met in New York City in a comparable and equitable manner.[17]

Confronted with this demarche, Donovan switched again, and on November 16, it was announced that a compromise ratio of one to 157
had been established for the private school programs for the coming
year. All told, the non-public-schools would be receiving about $3.2
million of the $15 million allocated to the city, and the editorial board
of the *Times* denounced the new move as

nothing less than a knuckling under to the church-school interests
of various denominations in this city. Instead of adhering to principle, the Board has played a numbers game in which the winning
figure was reached by satisfying the bargaining agents for the non-
public (parochial) schools. . . . it is incomprehensible how the
Board can justify giving non-public schools a *higher* [sic] ratio of
remedial reading teachers than it can offer in the public schools.[18]
[Emphasis in the original.]

On December 1, the NYCLU, the AJCongress, the United Federation of Teachers (the AFL–CIO local of New York City public school
teachers) and the United Parents Association announced that they were
challenging the constitutionality of the non-public-school remedial programs in both state and federal courts.

Into the Constitutional Arena

The lawyers of the major separationist groups had been determined
all along to test the constitutionality of the ESEA. Americans United,
always the fastest (but least accurate) gun among separationists, had
already initiated a challenge to Title I in Philadelphia, and to Title II
in Dayton. Even the moderate separationist groups which had agreed
to the Thompson formula wanted a constitutional ruling on the compromise now that it seemed to be breaking down in the implementation phase. Thus, after being defeated in the local politics of New
York City, the church-state professionals determined to constitutionalize the conflict and make the city's implementation of the ESEA the
national test.

In the federal suit it was alleged that sending teachers of remedial reading and arithmetic into private schools violated the establishment clause. The plaintiffs (federal taxpayers and parents of children in the city public schools) asked that the United States District Court for the Southern District of New York find either (1) that the city was implementing the Act in an unconstitutional fashion, or (2) that the Act itself was unconstitutional insofar as it authorized publicly financed instruction on private school premises.* But the crucial question presented by the case was standing. Leo Pfeffer who was directing the legal effort sponsored by the four groups, asked that *Frothingham v. Mellon* be reconsidered and that federal taxpayers be granted standing. At the very least he urged that an exception be made to the *Frothingham* rule for challenges to federal expenditures on establishment grounds.

The suit in state court was more complicated. It was an action by New York City taxpayers. While the State does not allow such suits against itself, the city does. In addition, one of the plaintiffs was the parent of city public school children, and two were remedial teachers who were eligible for duty in non-public-schools. On the merits of the issue it was alleged not only that New York City's implementation of ESEA violated the U.S. Constitution, but that New York City funds were being expended in the administration of the program, and thus the strict prohibition of aid to church schools by the New York Constitution was also breached. Certainly, city funds were being employed in administering the nonpublic remedial programs. Public employees spent their time planning them, and although every effort was made to keep local funds from being comingled with federal ones, these could not be handled without the city's incurring some overhead expenses.

The state suit has been postponed by stipulation of the parties, but the federal case has developed along certain very interesting lines. On June 19, 1967, a special three-judge district court (an arrangement reserved for suits challenging laws on federal constitutional grounds which provide direct review by the Supreme Court) dismissed the suit because the plaintiffs lacked standing. The vote was two to one, however, and the dissenting judge, Marvin E. Frankel, stressed the absurdity of a procedural rule which made it impossible for anyone to challenge a federal expenditure as a "law respecting an establishment of religion." Judge Frankel concluded that

---

*There were no exceptions to this constitutional attack. The backers of this suit are strict separationists and reject even the "welfare services" concept which the moderate separationists thought they had agreed to in 1965.

It seems perfectly obvious that those who wrote the First Amendment would have been astonished at the suggestion that it might come to be enforceable only against the states and not against the Federal Government.[19]

From Pfeffer's viewpoint this was an encouraging outcome; he could go to the Supreme Court with a strong lower court dissent in favor of his position.[20] In the fall of 1967, the Supreme Court agreed to hear the case *(Flast v. Gardner)* on the standing question and it was argued on March 12, 1968.*

ESEA and Race

As the conflict over the implementation of ESEA in New York City rose to a high heat further complications arose. We have noted the way in which the politics of race relations may intersect with the politics of church and state, and this is precisely what happened in New York.

Aryeh Neier, Executive Director of the New York Civil Liberties Union, brought the racial issue into the open on August 7, 1966, with the charge that New York's non-public-school enrollments were increasing rapidly because of middle-class escapees from public school integration.[21] This charge was quickly answered by several Catholic educators. Father Molloy declared that there was not a "shred of evidence to support that assertion."[22] In a letter to the *Times,* Monsignor Raymond P. Rigney, Superintendent of Schools of the Archdiocese of New York, offered figures which, he argued, refuted the charge that non-public-schools were profiting from integration tensions.[23] He pointed out that parochial school enrollments in Manhattan and the Bronx had declined slightly between 1965 and 1966, and that Catholic elementary schools in Manhattan enrolled 18,541 white children and 17,479 children "of Negro, Cuban, Puerto Rican, Latin-American and Oriental parentage," while in the Bronx the totals were 43,422 white to 11,008 others. These figures were widely quoted in the press, and they became the focus of debate at hearings held by the Platform Advisory of the State Republican Party where Father Molloy dueled with a NYCLU spokesman. In October, the Union formally responded to the Catholic counter-attack in a "public letter" from Neier pointing

---

*As was noted in the previous chapter, the Court did agree to standing, but the chances of the separationists winning on the *merits* were substantially reduced by the Court's decision, announced on the same day, in the New York textbook case.

out that Manhattan and the Bronx were not the world, and that in the city as a whole enrollments were rising in non-public-schools (25.4 percent of the total school population in 1950, 29.3 percent by 1960). Neier suggested that integration of Manhattan and Bronx parochial schools did not indicate integration of private schools generally, and he concluded that of the 400,000 children who attended Catholic schools in the City, and the almost 100,000 more who attended other nonpublic institutions, 90 percent were white.[24]

The New York NAACP and other Negro rights groups became active in the struggle over ESEA after the NYCLU brought the racial issue into focus, and it seems likely that a racial dimension has now been built into New York's continuing politics of church and state. Thus a difficult and already divisive conflict was made worse. Charges and counter-charges of bigotry reduce the capacity of group elites to bargain and accommodate, and increase the possibility that New York's normal political processes will be unable to compromise and "defuse" church-state conflicts.[25]

CONSTITUTIONAL REVISION

Governor Rockefeller's initiatives in education repeatedly triggered church-state squabbles, and the implementation of ESEA in the city deepened the New York conflict. But the major battle, which grew out of the others but became far more bitter and costly, involved the alteration of Article XI, Section 3, of the State Constitution. This was the ban on aid to church-related schools which had been at issue in the textbook case and in the second of the two judicial challenges to ESEA in New York City. Popularly known as the "Blaine Amendment," it commands that

> Neither the state nor any subdivision thereof shall use its property used, *directly* or *indirectly,* in aid or maintenance, other than for or credit or any public money, or authorize or permit either to be examination or inspection, of any school or institution of learning wholly or in part under the control or direction of any religious denomination, or in which any denominational tenet or doctrine is taught, but the legislature may provide for the transportation of children to and from any school or institution of learning. (Emphasis added.)

This is a stiff proscription. No one can mistake its intention—to keep church-related schools from benefiting in any way from any expenditure of public funds. The language was introduced into the New York Constitution in 1894, and if confirmation of its meaning is required, the history of that 1894 Convention is clear on the point. During the early 1890's there had been a surge of anti-Catholicism within the state's Protestant majority, and anxiety had increased over the support and patronage given to Roman Catholic schools, orphanages and hospitals by some local governments. But the Catholic hierarchy was not without political power, and in the pull and haul of convention politics a deal was done: a strict proscription of aid to church schools was included, but the Constitution left the way open for aid to welfare institutions.[26]

This was an accommodation which New York's Catholics have had cause to regret. In the 1890's, their hospitals and orphanages were getting more public support than their schools; protecting these former relationships with government had top priority. Today's Catholic educators manage a giant system which is caught in the usual cost squeeze. For them, and for most Catholics, education is now of primary concern while welfare has receded into the background.

The origin of the label "Blaine Amendment" for Article XI, Section 3, is interesting. In 1875, that prince of opportunists, James G. Blaine, Republican of Maine, then Speaker of the House of Representatives, introduced in Congress an amendment to the federal constitution which would have added to the language of the First Amendment a specific proscription of aid to church-related schools. The measure was, in part at least, an attempt to take advantage of an anti-Catholic ground swell in the mid-1870's to divert election-year attention from the scandals of the second Grant administration. In his unsuccessful campaign for the Presidency eight years later, Blaine fell victim to the volubility of a Presbyterian minister named Burchard who, in introducing the candidate to a gathering of New York supporters, referred to the Democrats as the party of "Rum, Romanism and Rebellion." Despite Blaine's later attempts to dissociate himself from such rhetoric, (he described Burchard as an "ass in the shape of a preacher"), "Blaine" became a symbol for anti-Catholicism in American politics.

The 1875 Amendment failed of passage, and there is no causal connection between it and the action of the New York Convention in 1894. The idea of specifically proscribing aid to church-related schools did not originate with Blaine; some states had included such proscriptions in their constitutions before 1875, and he died before the New Yorkers of 1894 made their constitution. Over the years, the enemies of Article XI, Section 3, have applied the label "Blaine" in an attempt to blacken it by association. And it cannot be denied that the same blend of separationist ideology and anti-Catholic animus which Blaine sought to mobilize nationally in 1875 was present in New York in 1894. To the extent that one wishes to identify Article XI, Section 3, with a common, and probably prevailing, nineteenth century separationist sentiment, the label may be defensible. In any case it has stuck.*

Support for a Constitutional Convention

By 1967 it was widely agreed among liberals in New York that revision of the state's basic law was long overdue. During the early 1960's, a number of interest groups committed themselves to the calling of a constitutional convention. Good-government organizations wanted a shorter, simpler constitution which would "get the judiciary out of politics." New York City interests were seeking to better the city's financial position by increasing its fiscal powers or shifting certain costs to the state's broader tax base. Groups representing Negroes and other low-income populations wanted broader powers accorded to the state for stimulating community development. Groups interested in capital-intensive projects (such as public housing) were hoping to eliminate the constitutional requirement for referenda on state bond issues. Governor Rockefeller and his aides wanted increased constitutional power to reorganize the executive branch of state government.

Especially among liberal Democrats there was a conviction that the existing charter, which had its last thoroughgoing revision in 1894, was too long, too encumbered with complicated and trivial amendments, and too restrictive of the state power. New York, it was argued, was entering a period in which state government would necessarily be assuming more responsibilities. The problems of the state were held to be forcing the governor and the legislature into ever increasing policy innovation, and such "positive government" required new constitutional underpinning. Finally, in November 1965, the state's voters were coaxed into approving a constitutional convention for the spring of 1967, with delegates to be elected in November of 1966.

Getting a new constitution, however, would require that the state's political processes—its processes of bargaining and conciliation—work at something approaching their best. Numerous potentially clashing interests were involved, and since any new charter would have to be

*And of course Article XI, Section 3 is not an "amendment" but a regular article.

approved by a majority of the voters, a carefully built coalition would
be needed to overcome the conservatism of many parts of the state's
electorate which would oppose any increase in governmental powers.
In such a delicate business, the interjection of one highly disruptive
issue might make the political task impossible. Aid to church-related
schools was potentially such an issue, and accommodationists were determined to seize the opportunity for the repeal of the Blaine
Amendment.

The legislature established a Temporary State Commission for the
Revision and Simplification of the Constitution which was to hold
hearings, do research, prepare materials and air the important issues
which would come before the delegates. Hearings before the Temporary Commission began in October of 1966, and ran through the fall
election campaign in which delegates to the coming convention were
chosen and Governor Rockefeller stood for re-election. Soon after the
hearings got underway, the Commission Chairman declared that three
major issues were emerging: home rule (fiscal powers) for New York
City, judicial reform and church-state relations. One exchange before
the Temporary Commission is typical of many which took place during
this period concerning the Blaine Amendment. J. Eugene McMahon,
Treasurer of Catholic Charities in Buffalo, told the Commissioners that
the "rights of parents and children have been frustrated by this unfortunate constitutional relic." The Reverend Arthur W. Meilke, pas-
tor of the First Presbyterian Church of Buffalo (and member of the
National Advisory Council of Americans United) followed McMahon
to the witness chair and responded that the principle of separation was
"threatened by the Roman Catholic Church, which would modify our
State Constitution to make possible tax support of parochial schools."[27]
A total of 29 nongovernmental witnesses spoke on Article XI, Section
3; 15 advocated repeal and 14 retention or strengthening of the provision. By the end of 1966, it was generally recognized that the church-
state issue would prove the most difficult and divisive with which the
189 delegates would have to deal the following spring.[28] To the state's
cost, this proved to be the case.

The Gubernatorial Campaign

The 1966 gubernatorial race accelerated the conflict over Blaine. On
October 5, 1966, Governor Rockefeller, "drumming up votes along
the Mohawk," addressed the students of Bishop Scully High School, in
Schenectady. "Stepping gingerly around the emotion-charged issue of

state aid to church schools," he told his audience that "we all recognize the problem. The question is how to deal with this within the basic traditions of the community."[29] A week later, Professor Paul Adams, the candidate of the Conservative Party (a reactionary faction attempting to establish a position as a make-weight between the major parties), announced that he opposed all aid to church-related schools. Then, apparently realizing that this would not do for the candidate of a party which hoped to draw support from New York's many conservative Catholics, he hastily added that he would support tax credits for tuition fees paid private schools.[30] And the issue was further dramatized when Franklin D. Roosevelt, Jr., candidate of the Liberal Party (a "lib-lab" analogue to the Conservatives) declared himself opposed to any change in Article XI, Section 3. He argued that great amounts of money would flow to private schools if the constitutional barrier were lowered and that this could better be spent on public schools. This was, he concluded, "the same fight my mother made against Cardinal Spellman in 1949."[31]

With Rockefeller waffeling, and Roosevelt drawing the praise of the editorial board of the *Times* for his unequivocal stand, speculation centered on the course that the Democratic candidate Frank O'Connor would take. On October 18, the New York Civil Liberties Union released the returns on a church-state questionnaire sent to Rockefeller, Roosevelt and O'Connor. Rockefeller ignored the question regarding revision of Blaine; Roosevelt took his announced position; O'Connor replied that the State did not need a church-state provision more restrictive than the federal First Amendment, and promised a position paper on the matter. Three days later, that paper was released. It attacked Rockefeller for being "less than honest" on the issue of aid to church-related schools, and explained that "the language of the Federal Bill of Rights has served us as a nation for nearly two hundred years." O'Connor concluded by supporting "limited and appropriate" aid to children in non-public-schools.[32] In short, he plumped for repeal of the Blaine Amendment. The Governor responded by accusing O'Connor of taking a "completely ambiguous" position, and announced that the whole problem needed more study.[33]

The relationship between New York's voting patterns and the stands of the candidates on revision of Article XI, Section 3, is worth noting.[34] Governor Rockefeller, wishing to be rid of Blaine, could not be too militant about the matter because of the need to hold traditionally Republican voters in the upstate Protestant countryside. Roosevelt, whose natural constituency as a Liberal candidate was urban and heavily Jewish, could take a hard separationist line which fit his personal predilections. Frank O'Connor, who knew he would be made or broken by his support in the City's heavily Catholic Democratic organizations, went for repeal.

Interest Group Activity

The professional church-state groups were now deeply involved in New York, and they did not restrict their activities to testifying before the Temporary Commission. At the beginning of the battle the accommodationists stole a march and were very effective in the electoral process.

Seeing New York as a crucial test case for aid to private schools, the Citizens for Educational Freedom established an office in Manhattan and held forums in 55 senatorial districts of the State during the last weeks of the 1966 campaign with candidates for delegateships invited to express their views on Article XI, Section 3. Every would-be delegate was queried by CEF as to his views on Blaine, and plans were laid to have a full-time lobbyist at the convention when it opened in the spring.[35] Many delegates from heavily Catholic districts afterward recalled this early CEF pressure as hard to withstand, and there were frequent reports of threats that if a delegate went wrong on Blaine, a terrible vengeance would be worked when he next stood for elective office.

Charles Tobin, Director of the New York Catholic Welfare Conference, was in continuous communication with prospective leaders of the convention; Father Molloy and his Committee of Independent School Officials (switching their attention from ESEA implementation) issued press releases; and the National Jewish Commission on Law and Public Affairs also moved into the Blaine Amendment propaganda in a small way. Individual members of the Catholic hierarchy, and especially the Chancellery of Cardinal Spellman's Archdiocese of New York, made public professions and private representations for repeal. The *Tablet*, weekly organ of the Catholic Diocese of Brooklyn, announced on November 10, 1966, that its polling showed 106 of the 186 delegates already committed to the revision of Article XI, Section 3.

In addition to the usual accommodationist and non-public-school actors, several of the state's private universities joined in the effort to alter Article XI, Section 3. As a spokesman for New York University put it, "It will be practically impossible to get funds for private schools like N.Y.U., unless Fordham can get them, too."[36]

Inevitably, Leo Pfeffer's was the first prominent separationist voice raised in warning. In an article in *Christian Century*, in July of 1966 (when most amateur and professional separationists in New York were preoccupied with the textbook law and ESEA implementation), Pfeffer strongly supported Article XI, Section 3, scolded the NCC for accepting the ESEA compromise which he thought encouraged Catholic ambitions, and identified the retention of Blaine as the crucial church-state issue for New York and the nation for the coming year.[37] As early as May of 1966 Pfeffer had begun holding informal meetings of separationists to discuss possible strategies.[38]

In the fall of 1966 Americans United entered the fray. AU issued a pamphlet entitled *Wake Up New York*. This was followed by an "Emergency Alert" letter to "members and friends" outlining the "constitutional crisis" in New York and asking funds for a campaign of resistance. A large portion of the December, 1966, issue of *Church and State,* the Americans United house organ, was devoted to New York political and religious issues. It identified Cardinal Spellman as the villain of the piece, and called for all separationist groups to meet and shape a common New York strategy.

Of course a common strategy was already being developed, with Leo Pfeffer and the AJCongress taking the lead. AU had been excluded from these councils because of its recklessness and its perceived anti-Catholicism. It was not felt that the united separationist front in New York should be quite that united. In early 1967 the decision was taken to formalize the organization of cooperating groups by establishing the Committee for Public Education and Religious Liberty (PEARL), which would serve as a clearing house for activity in defense of Article XI, Section 3, and, under its director William Haddad, become a group actor in its own right.[39] This single-issue "super group" had 24 members including the NYCLU, the United Parents Association, the United Federation of Teachers (all sponsors of the New York City ESEA suits) and others such as the American Jewish Committee, the Protestant Council of New York City, the Americans for Democratic Action and the Anti-Defamation League.

PEARL issued figures purporting to show that it would cost less to absorb New York State's 800,000-plus Roman Catholic parochial school pupils into the public school system than to give any public support to the parochial system. This argument was supposedly pre-

dicated on the experience of certain Southern states which have experi-
mented with aid to private schools. The conclusion was labeled "nonsense" and the reasoning denounced as "dishonest" by a spokesman of
the Archdiocese of New York.[40] PEARL also communicated with delegates and with leaders of the convention, and developed a strategy
which its leaders hoped might save the day for Article XI, Section 3.

It was during this period, early 1967, that the long-range strategy
of the cooperating separationists began to jell. The crucial variable in
their plans was the fashion in which the new constitution would be
put before the state's voters.

Whatever the convention produced had to be approved by a referendum at the November election in 1967. It was possible, however, for
various provisions of the new constitution to be "parceled out" and
presented to the electorate as separate questions. If the new charter
were submitted as a single package, anyone who deeply opposed one
provision would be forced to vote against the whole. If provisions
were parceled out, the voter could approve the new constitution except
for the part—perhaps revision of the Blaine Amendment—which
troubled him. While not accepting the *Tablet* poll as strictly accurate,
separationist strategists quickly realized that while they could make a
morale-boosting fight at the convention, they could not win. After sur-
veying the delegates, they understood that Article XI, Section 3, was
going to be changed and that the language of the federal First
Amendment would be substituted. The early work of the accommodationists had seen to that. But if separationists could force "single
submission," it was quite possible that the separationist votes, along
with the votes of opponents of other new provisions, would be enough
to defeat the entire package. Thus, the strict separationists hoped to
doom one constitutional innovation by dooming them all.

The importance of the submission question was attested to by calls
for the parceling out of Blaine from groups and individuals princi-
pally concerned with the reform and shortening of the old constitution. These groups wanted the church-state issue and other highly
controversial matters to be voted on separately, so that the provisions
they were interested in could be considered on their own merits. Just
before the delegates assembled, for instance, the Committee on Constitutional Issues, an ad hoc group of reformers known to be close to
the office of Senator Robert Kennedy (D., N.Y.) declared that Article
XI, Section 3, was a problem so delicate and divisive that unless special precautions were taken, it might frustrate all efforts to achieve
constitutional revision.[41]

Throughout the struggle over the proposed constitution, the editorial board of the *Times* vigorously supported the retention of Blaine. On March 29, the board announced that "for well over a century, New York State has followed the principle that its citizens are free to send their children either to public or private schools, but that tax moneys can be expended only on public schools."[42] On July 13, as the convention battle over Article XI, Section 3, approached, New Yorkers were reminded that alteration would be a "retrograde step" which "would weaken the fundamental policy of separation of church and state and seriously endanger the public school system."[43]

All across the state, interest rose. During the spring and summer of 1967 many sermons were preached demanding justice for parochial schools or continuance of the "American way in church and state." On Sunday, July 2, for instance, radio station WABC carried a lengthy "editorial" on the subject, which identified Blaine as the most important issue before the convention, and urged listeners to obtain the names of their delegates and to write expressing their views. Many other radio and TV stations followed suit. Some, such as WCBS-TV in New York City followed the editorial lead of the *Times* and supported the retention of Blaine. As the time for convention decision on Article XI, Section 3, approached, a far wider audience than usually follows the politics of church and state looked with intense interest toward Albany and the delegates in the State Assembly Chamber of the State House.

"Governmental" Interest Group Activity

One fascinating feature of the battle over Article XI, Section 3, was the way in which governmental agencies within the state divided on the issues and took sides publicly.

In his testimony before the Temporary Commission, Dr. James E. Allen, New York's Commissioner of Education, stated that it was "ridiculous" for the state to have in its constitution a provision which seemed more restrictive of aid to church-related schools than the federal constitution. Such a dualism, Allen said, created serious legal and administrative difficulties for his department—state and federal funds could not be comingled, and this necessitated extra bookkeeping. All this was a tiresome hindrance and got in the way of the important business of education in the state.[44] Thus, the State Department of Education was firmly committed to repeal of Blaine.

On May 26, 1967, the Board of Regents of the State of New York, Allen's immediate overseers, met in an unusual and hastily arranged session in a Plattsburgh hotel before going on to Montreal for a tour of Expo '67. Pressure had been mounting for the Regents to make some statement on Blaine, and a rare split occurred at the Plattsburgh meeting. A majority of 10 backed Allen and the Department of Education, calling for substitution of the language of the First Amendment for Article XI, Section 3. A minority of 5 (including the one Negro Regent, Kenneth Clark, and a former President of the New York City Board of Education, Max Rubin) supported retention of Blaine. It could not have been an altogether happy tour of Expo, for there is every indication that feelings within the group ran deep. On July 23, as the convention hesitantly approached the church-state issue, Max Rubin publicly re-emphasized the position of the Regents minority, and spoke of the need to reduce "another form of segregation— segregation by religion."[45]

The position of the New York City educational establishment was just the reverse of that taken by the state Department of Education. During the spring of 1967, many public school teachers, with the approval of principals and superintendents, passed out to their pupils materials prepared by the United Parents Association. These were to be taken home to the parents, and they included a statement of opposition to any change in Article XI, Section 3, which was to be signed and returned to the teacher by the child for forwarding to convention delegates. When this practice was vigorously criticized by officials of the Archdiocese of New York and the Diocese of Brooklyn, public school officials explained that it was settled policy for teachers to pass out materials at the request of PTA's and that the United Parents Association materials had come into the school system in this way.[46] All pretenses were dropped, however, on July 19, when the Board of Education announced that the repeal of Article XI, Section 3, "would permit an erosion of the public school system."[47] Catholic teachers protested, but the Board weighed in on the separationist side.

The leaders of the state Department of Education apparently felt some of the Governor's concern for "all the children of the state," and their objective—their "success indicator," if you will—with regard to federal programs such as ESEA was to secure for New York as large a total sum as possible. The city Board of Education, on the other hand, was preoccupied with the public schools in its charge, and with getting as much as possible for them out of any outside aid which became available. The opposing positions on Blaine seem to have grown directly out of these basic differences in orientation.

The Dynamics of the Convention

From the opening gavel a clear majority existed within the Demo-cratic-controlled convention for scrapping the Blaine Amendment. Catholic delegates were almost solidly for repeal, and Protestants and Jews from the Brooklyn, Queens and Bronx Democratic organizations were under heavy pressure to go along. As Andrew Hacker later pointed out, two-thirds of the Jewish delegates came out for repeal, but almost all of these were Democratic party stalwarts from the out-lying boroughs of New York City where the parochial schools are strong and the relations between the Roman Catholic Church and the "regular" Democratic organizations are cordial.[48] Most of the votes for retaining Blaine came from liberal Democratic delegates from "re-form" organizations in Manhattan, and from upstate Republican Prot-estants. The final tally for repeal was 131 to 50.

The debate over Blaine began with a packed gallery and extra guards. The Reverend Donald S. Harrington, State Chairman of the Liberal Party (and member of Americans United's National Advisory Council) was the most passionate opponent of repeal, but passion only served to increase bitterness and harden positions. As one dele-gate put it, "these guys have been waiting more than four months to stand up and talk about this, but I don't think any of the debate will change anybody's mind."[49] Rhetoric soared, and as the debate drew to a close, another delegate, fearing the divisive potential of the issue, rose and asked his fellows "why in heaven's name jeopardize what we are striving for and possibly the entire new constitution by not joining in a sensible [compromise] solution?"[50] It was a very good question.

The separationists, in fact, did not go away empty-handed. They achieved an important concession in the form of a guarantee in the new charter giving citizens the right to challenge any state expenditure on constitutional grounds. This was significant as taxpayer suits had not previously been allowed at the state level. In addition, it was pro-vided that no school or other institution being aided by the state could discriminate on religious grounds. This would have required that church schools accept students of all denominations as a condition of aid. Yet few opponents of Blaine repeal were appeased. After the sub-stitution of the First Amendment language (the Legislature shall make no law respecting an establishment of religion, or prohibiting the free exercise thereof), strict separationist interest group representatives girded themselves for an electoral fight to the death.

Yet the most important fact about Blaine for Convention President

Anthony Travia, leader of the Democratic delegates, was that Catholics seemed to care passionately about repealing it and that they made up approximately 40 percent of the state's population. Even though Protestant and Jewish organizations were opposed, and some Protestant delegates grumbled, it did not seem from the vantage point of Albany that pro-Blaine sentiment ran anywhere near as deep within the electorate as anti-Blaine sentiment.

To Travia, upstate Protestants were a hopeless lot anyway. They were generally Republican, economically conservative (one provision of the new charter which was taking shape would have widened the State's borrowing powers), and they were suspicious of *any* change. As one Democratic delegate put it, "they would vote against a new constitution whether we kept Blaine or not, but Catholics, even Republican Catholics, are so eager to kill Blaine that they'll go for the whole constitution even though they may not like some other features."

This "Catholic strategy" lay behind Travia's decision to offer the new charter as a single package. He was gambling that many who might otherwise have voted against the constitution would support it because of the Blaine repeal, and that relatively few who would otherwise have supported the convention's product would turn away on church-state grounds. Travia hoped to save the work of the convention, but if his assessment of Catholic rank-and-file commitment to the Blaine repeal was wrong, it would doom the new charter beyond hope of salvage. Travia was standing the separationist strategy on its head! They meant to beat the whole constitution by adding their "No" votes to others against a single package. Travia meant to overcome the "No" votes of economic conservatives by "locking in" a heavy Catholic "Yes" vote on a single package. On the final convention vote on submission Travia was three votes short of the number required to carry his single-submission scheme. He got these needed votes from David Dubinsky, Alex Rose and Donald Harrington—the three Liberal Party delegates who had led the separationist floor fight for retention of Blaine.

The Campaign on the Constitution

In the preconvention and convention phases of the Blaine battle, accommodationist forces had had things very much their own way. Charles Tobin of the New York Catholic Conference lobbied the convention effectively—speaking, it was said, with the full authority of the State's bishops.[51] While separationists tend to be most aggressive in the constitutional arena, accommodationists often seize the initiative

in state and local arenas, and especially so when their ends can be
served through work with party organizations and in the electoral process. The close ties of the New York City Democracy to the Roman
Catholic hierarchy together with CEF's threats of voter retaliation combined to give the accommodationists their early advantage. Separationist groups were concentrating on protests and court tests of the Rockefeller textbook law and the ESEA, while CEF was convincing the men
who were going to write the new constitution that broad sentiment
existed for the repeal of Blaine, and that the opposition consisted
mainly of bigots, Godless hyperliberals and the editorial board of the
Times.

With the close of the convention, however, the advantage began to
shift. One after another the most prestigious liberal groups within the
state denounced the repeal of Blaine and the single submission. Where
early in the convention the specialized separationist groups and the
Liberal Party had borne the brunt of combat against the accommodationists, now a whole squadron of "good-government forces" came to
the rescue. The New York Citizens Union, the City Club of New York
City, the League of Women Voters and the Episcopal Diocese of New
York were only a few of those that attacked the convention's leaders
for altering Blaine. Through the spring and summer the convention
had been getting a rather unfavorable press ("do-nothing" and "politically dominated" led among the accusations), and liberals were now
able to fix on Blaine repeal as a clear case of the capitulation of "party
politicos" to clerical pressure for aid to church schools.

Indeed, the church-state issue had such emotional power over liberals
that it virtually eclipsed the seemingly dull, compromise-ridden work
of the convention. Blaine repeal touched a highly sensitive nerve within many of the very groups which had supported the calling of a convention and worked hard for the cause of a new constitution. They
turned on the convention and denounced it as a sellout of the people
by Democratic party hacks.* The Blaine issue was prominently publicized all through the convention. Now other newspapers and broad-
casters joined the *Times* in taking a strict separationist stand. Espe-

---

*It is true that good-government groups suffered other disappointments at the
hands of the delegates. There was no reform of the judiciary and no new home-
rule taxing powers for New York City. Judging from behavior during the constitutional campaign, however, the church-state issue was crucial to their defection. As one strict-separationist leader remarked, "this is a gut issue for them;
there is a lot of overlapping membership between those organizations and ours."

cially in New York City, Blaine's defenders used their high prestige and previous commitment to constitutional reform to propagandize effectively for the defeat of Travia's package. *Christianity and Crisis* was one of the few liberal publications to support Blaine repeal.

While the Blaine battle held the New York City headlines and the attention of many liberals, powerful forces were moving against the proposed constitution (as Travia had known they would) for reasons quite unrelated to church-state relations. The Conservative Party and most Republican leaders denounced it as a spender's charter which would mean higher taxes. In upstate New York it was tagged as a "bag of goodies" for New York City, and this theme was hammered home by Republican newspaper editors. The forces of economic conservatism and provincialism operated in much less visible ways than did the friends and foes of Blaine. Yet in one respect their indictment coincided with that of those who were outraged by the proposed repeal of Blaine: the convention had been composed of hack politicians who had given in to pressure—pressure from the Catholic hierarchy according to the supporters of Blaine, pressure from vaguely identified "spenders" and from New York City,* according to the Republicans and other economic conservatives.

In vain a few voices warned that anti-social-welfare and antiurban elements were mounting an unopposed scare campaign against the economic provisions of the proposed constitution. Preserving Blaine was the issue of the hour for most of New York's liberal groups and leaders, and paralyzed those who were the natural enemies of economic conservatism. Within a matter of weeks opposition to the new constitution on church-state grounds became a mark of liberal orthodoxy in the state.

Suddenly on the defensive (with the convention battle won but the constitutional war increasingly in doubt), Citizens for Educational Freedom counterattacked. With funds supplied from outside its own ranks, CEF launched an elaborate propaganda campaign of full-page newspaper advertisements and radio and TV spots urging a "Yes" vote on Travia's package. Ads showed private school students laboring under various difficulties which, it was suggested, were caused by, or could not be ministered to because of, Article XI, Section 3. Separa-

---

*As Professor James Crouthamel of Hobart College (Geneva, New York) ruefully remarked just after the campaign, "up here the great enemy of Western civilization is not Peking, it is New York City."

tionists challenged the veracity of these ads, the nastiness of charges and counter-charges increased, and there was even an announcement by PEARL that CEF had introduced a paid spy into its office staff— hotly denied by CEF. Parochial school students rang doorbells throughout the state urging "Yes" votes, and many newly activated separationists predicted anti-Catholic backlash.

THE SIGNIFICANCE OF THE BLAINE AMENDMENT

In order to appreciate fully the implications of the battle over the words of Article XI, Section 3, it is necessary to step back from the narrative at this point, and ask the elementary, but very important question: just what was at stake in the battle over repeal of the Blaine Amendment? Over what were New Yorkers actually fighting? The answer involves legal, political and emotional factors.

Legally, Article XI, Section 3, had the potential of committing New York to a stricter separation of church and state than that required by the United States Supreme Court under the federal constitution. In *Everson,* the Supreme Court opened the way for the "individual-benefit theory" of the establishment clause, with its distinction between direct and indirect aid. While the Court has not yet clearly accepted this approach, much less specified ground rules for determining what is direct or indirect, it is likely that it eventually will adopt some version of "individual benefit." This is the assumption on which church-school partisans are banking. But the Blaine Amendment specifically proscribes both direct and indirect aid. If it were retained, the argument went, there would be types of aid permissible under the federal constitution but outlawed in New York. The difficulty with this argument was that the New York Court of Appeals had shown little disposition to take Blaine seriously. In the *East Greenbush* textbook case (which was decided well before the convention decided on Blaine), a majority of the Court had agreed to the virtual gutting of the provision. Judge Scileppi's opinion for the Court was so permissive as to allow almost any aid unless the state was purposely attempting to support the religious activities of church schools or was discriminating between denominations in giving aid.[52] Given the care with which political and ethnic balances are maintained on the New York Court of Appeals, it is doubtful whether a new majority will form which will read life into Blaine. Thus it is difficult to see that keeping or scrapping Article XI made much legal difference at all.

Politically, Blaine was significant to the extent that its fate might affect the posture of the state's leaders toward the church-related schools. Governor Rockefeller, for instance, had shown himself favorably disposed toward church-related schools. He had even announced himself ready to appoint a commission to study the forms future aid might take—*if* Blaine were repealed. However, should the new constitution fail of adoption, and should the circumstances of its failure indicate substantial voter resistance to church-school aid, it was argued that the Governor and other policy makers would leave the church schools to go it alone for a long time to come. Even though Blaine's presence in the Constitution might be of doubtful legal significance, it was suggested that it had an inhibiting effect. But again, less was at stake than seemed to be at first glance. The legislative leaders of both parties had already pledged themselves to greater help for church schools. They had also pledged themselves to the eventual repeal of Blaine, regardless of the fate of Travia's constitutional package. A rather good case could be made that the defeat of the new charter would not stop the development of programs of aid to church schools; that at most it would only slow the process down a bit.

It is only when one turns to the psychological significance of Blaine that it becomes fully clear why the question of its repeal generated such intense heat. In the cases of Rockefeller's textbook program and of ESEA implementation in New York City, certain specific sums of money were at stake. But the "dollars-and-cents" meaning of Blaine (its legal and political significances) paled beside its importance as a symbol. To Catholic leaders the self-respect of the Catholic community in New York seemed to demand repeal. If not, the evidence of the humiliating 1894 bargain would remain as a kind of standing "status insult"—a constant reminder of the past WASP domination of the state and of past Catholic inferiority. The courts and the legislature might render Article XI, Section 3, nugatory, but this would not be nearly as satisfying as eliminating it cleanly and openly in a referendum. It is not very satisfying to destroy a symbol in the dark. For the separationist groups and their temporary liberal allies, Blaine had the same emotionally electrifying effect. The convention was rife with rumors of pressure from the "hierarchy." There was dark talk of clerical domination and the destruction of the public school system. Underlying antipathies toward Catholics became manifest, and a kind of "Armageddon Now" attitude became widespread. Many supporters of Blaine insisted on discussing the issue as if it represented a proposal for the state to pick up the total bill for running church-related schools. It did no good for the observer to inquire into the extent to which preserving Blaine would actually keep money away from church-related schools. It seemed vital to many separationists to prevent Blaine repeal so that accommodationist forces would be kept in their place.

The Reckoning

On Election Day Eve, the interest group forces contending over the new constitution were arrayed roughly as follows: conservative and upstate groups working hard and relying on the antispending reflexes of middle-class voters to defeat the new constitution; liberal groups opposing the new constitution and pointing to the retention of Blaine as the only issue; accommodationist groups favoring the new constitution and pointing to the repeal of Blaine as the only issue (but greatly worried over whether middle-class Catholics would vote as Catholics or as economic conservatives). The leadership of Negro and Puerto Rican communities were split. Minority group spokesmen such as Bronx Borough President Herman Badillo had worked hard to get liberal economic provisions into the proposed charter and supported it vigorously. Many Negro leaders did the same, including all ten Negro delegates to the convention. But the New York NAACP denounced the repeal of Blaine as a sellout of the public schools, and certain highly visible Negro militants, such as the Reverend Milton Galamison, took a similar line.[53]

Besides the accommodationists, the only groups to hold fast for the new constitution were the regular democratic organizations (clubs) of New York City which had dominated the convention (and many of these only went through the motions of support). Among the reform democratic clubs there was substantial support of Blaine, with some clubs actively working for the constitution's defeat.

As it turned out, accommodationist leaders were justified in worrying about how middle-class Catholics would vote. The constitutional package was rejected 1,309,897 to 3,364,630. Upstate and in the suburbs the vote was over 3 to 1 against, and this was reduced only to 2 to 1 against in New York City. This was a stinging defeat for the regular Democrats and the leaders of the convention who had fought for its product. The results in the city were especially dramatic. Not only did liberal Jewish Assembly Districts go against the proposed constitution, but so did middle-class Catholic A.D.'s. Areas of Queens and Brooklyn with high Catholic populations turned in substantial "No" votes. Only the poor went for the new constitution. Two out of three A.D.'s in Harlem supported the package, and in the third the vote was close. In Brooklyn, a few "depressed" districts such as Greenpoint and Brownsville-Bedford-Stuyvesant voted approval, and in the Bronx, two districts with high concentrations of Puerto Ricans also voted "Yes." No Queens district was carried by the constitutional package, but the voting was closest in low-income areas.

It is clear that the church-state issue did not defeat the proposed constitution—it only helped. The electoral decision seems to have represented a middle-class rejection of what appeared a "spenders" charter. Despite the public positions taken by almost every Catholic group from the Archdiocese of New York to the Catholic firemen, the Catholic lawyers and the Knights of Columbus, large numbers of Catholics voted "No"—especially in the suburbs.

But the vote against the constitution could not have been as large if liberal groups had not become caught up in a last-ditch defense of Blaine. The church-state conflict so monopolized the attention of the liberals, and so befogged the public discussion of the proposed constitution, that any chance of overcoming the "standing conservatism" of major portions of the New York electorate was quickly sacrificed. It is interesting that many Catholics were unwilling to vote "Yes," but there could be no surprise in the rejection of a document opposed by both the New York Chapter of Americans For Democratic Action and the Richmond (Staten Island) Taxpayers Association.

In the wake of the defeat of the proposed constitution there was a good deal of highly publicized talk by the leaders of both parties about taking its "good" provisions and passing them piecemeal as amendments to the existing charter.[54] This would require the passage of particular proposals in successive sessions of the legislature, and then their approval by a majority of the voters. The only "good" provision on which the party leaders could agree, however, was repeal of the Blaine Amendment. The Republicans, who controlled the State Senate and thus had a stranglehold on the amending process, declared that the liberal economic provisions of the proposed charter were clearly not "good," and argued that it would be an insult to the people to resubmit them. The regular Democrats, led by Anthony Travia, now in his capacity as Speaker of the Assembly, took the position that the people had been "sold a bill of goods," that the vote was not a true test of sentiment on Blaine and that the liberal economic provisions would be

pushed through. Privately, however, several prominent regular Democrats commented on the bleak prospect for getting anything before the
people in the forseeable future except Blaine repeal. One liberal Democratic leader advocated the appointment by the Governor of a blue-
ribbon commission to attempt to get the church-state issue out of politics so that liberals could concentrate on "educating" the public in the
subtleties of constitutional reform. His, however, was very much a
voice in the wilderness. Separationists were heady with "victory" and
accommodationists were sore; both were ready to go again.

The church-state conflict in New York in 1967 wrenched the normal political structure of the State far out of alignment. It pre-empted
the energies of liberal elites and gave conservative elites a free hand
in opposing the proposed constitution. It raised the emotional level of
much of the discussion of the constitution to the point of shrillness,
and decreased its clarity proportionally. Finally, it has left a legacy of
bitterness and suspicion among Catholic and non-Catholic New Yorkers
which will be a factor in the politics of the State for years to come
even if the battle over Blaine is somehow ended.

Furthermore, the church-state news from other parts of the nation
was not very encouraging in the fall of 1967. In September the *Times*
reported that the Governor of Pennsylvania had been forced to cut
short a trade-mission trip to Europe because of the intensity of conflict
over a bill before his Legislature which would involve the state in
supporting church-related schools.[55] In New Hampshire, part of the
income of the state's lottery was set aside to aid hard-pressed church-
related schools, and this was immediately challenged in court by the
Civil Liberties Union, the AJCongress and the National Council of
Churches (its first major litigation).[56] Half a dozen states were
troubled over arrangements for bussing children to church-related
schools. The cost of the politics of church and state have been high
for New York, and there is no reason to believe these costs atypical.

CHAPTER FIVE

THE CHURCH-
STATE PROSPECT

W hat kind of summing up can be made? We have surveyed the sources of church-state tensions, examined the principal group actors, noted the distinctive features and interrelations of the areas of conflict, and observed how church-state conflict has recently intensified in New York. The politics of church and state has been portrayed as a professionalized group politics at the top (in the constitutional and national policy-making arenas) which opens up at the bottom (in the state and local arena) to admit amateurs who are ferociously but only temporarily aroused. It has also been suggested that while church-state conflicts are problematical for political leaders and innovators in social policy, they do not possess the destructive potential of racial conflicts.

The danger is that as government, and especially the Federal Government, becomes more active in financing education and welfare programs, church-state issues will arise more frequently and intersect with racial issues more often. And church-state conflicts can reach high temperatures and be profoundly divisive. As James S. Coleman has pointed out, individuals and groups dispute most bitterly in the absence of psychological cross pressures and conflicting loyalties, and

> This is one reason that conflict between religious groups, as conflict between national groups, has often been of considerable intensity. Members of a religious group feel little cross pressure when faced with a conflict between their religious group and another.[1]

When religious identifications and beliefs are at the root of a political struggle it is extremely difficult to compromise the matter through the normal political bargaining. Peter Drucker has suggested that part of the strength of the American political system lies in its capacity to reduce political conflicts to economical conflicts—to disputes over dollars and cents. Referring to the "political economists of the American tradition," Drucker wrote that

> Above all, they saw that economic conflict was the one clash within the body politic that could be managed. It could be managed because economic interests are divisible whereas political or religious beliefs are not. One can always split an economic difference in two— and while half a loaf is better than no bread, half a child, as King Solomon long ago perceived, is not good at all. The same goes for half a religion . . .[2]

The danger of the politics of church and state is precisely that it tends to resist reduction to bargaining over shares. While some difference-splitting is done, the ideological component tends to be distressingly large. This would indicate that if substantial numbers of people continue to respond to the cues of the separationist and accommodationist interest groups, we can expect further instances in which, as in the defeat of President Kennedy's aid to education proposals and the defeat of the proposed New York constitution, the processes of political innovation are impeded or frozen by church-state conflicts.

Are more or less people likely to respond to the interest group cues? With the trigger issues arising more frequently and in ever more pressing forms, the future clearly depends on the underlying sources of church-state conflict. If they weaken, popular sensitivities will be dulled and pragmatic adjustments will be worked out on the trigger issues. If the underlying sources persist or increase, we are in for trouble. In describing the underlying sources of church-state conflict in Chapter I, I intimated that they were declining. It must be admitted, however, that there is evidence both ways.

TOWARD FREQUENT STALEMATE

Church-state politics in the constitutional and national policy-making arenas has been, thus far, an affair of professionals; only occasionally has it elicited a mass response (e.g., Truman's nomination of Mark Clark as Ambassador to the Vatican). For this reason it has been limited in its intensity and troublesomeness. In state and local arenas conflict has been less professionalized, usually intermittent, badly focused,

THE POLITICS OF RELIGIOUS CONFLICT

and insufficiently dramatic to hold the attention or engage the emotions of many people for very long. Again, intensity and troublesomeness have been limited. Yet in New York in 1967, a church-state conflict became so intense, and such large sectors of the public became sensitized to the issue, that a major governmental innovation, a new constitution, was imperiled. On its face, this event suggests at least the persistence, if not the amplification of the sources of church-state tension. And there are other signs which can be read as pointing in this direction.

The Southern Baptists, traditional carriers of "pure" Protestant separationist doctrine (and of considerable anti-Catholicism), are the fastest growing Protestant denomination. They now number eleven million, and fire-eating separationist pronouncements continue to issue from many of their leaders.[3] While no sure conclusion can be drawn from this, it is at least arguable that the value of strict separation is being reinforced for this increasing segment of the population. If so, the tension-producing implications are obvious. In addition to the Southern Baptists, certain pentecostal and fundamentalist sects (what Henry P. Van Dusen once called the "Third Force" in American Christianity) have been growing rapidly.[4] Including the Jehovah's Witnesses and the Seventh Day Adventists, the Third Force tends to be militantly separationist and often anti-Roman.

On the accommodationist side, Catholic demands are clearly intensifying, and there appears to be declining willingness to hold back for fear of provoking conflict. In the past many Catholic leaders spoke of support for their educational and welfare operations, but they also spoke of the impracticality of forcing issues and the wisdom of settling for relatively modest gains from the public sector. Today the characteristic call (especially where aid for education is concerned) is for parity; the parochial school student gets whatever is going to his public school peer.

The Catholic community now encompasses roughly 25 percent of our population—about 46,000,000 Americans. It has a tremendous investment in a school system which is under severe financial pressure, and which will eventually have to be scaled down if excluded from all public programs. A decision not to aid Catholic parochial schools is seen increasingly as a sentence of mutilation and possibly of death-by-degrees. A stern arithmetic of costs is held to underlie the warning issued by the Catholic Conference of Pennsylvania in August, 1967, that without aid many parochial school students would have to be transferred into public schools causing a "grave disturbance" and tax increase.[5] It is no accident, for instance, that Citizens for Educational Freedom has grown so fast and takes such a militant line.

In addition to these signs of increasing church-state sensitivity among Protestants and Catholics, the growth of an increasingly aggressive secularism may also be noted. This is much in evidence among the young, liberal, highly educated, first-generation professionals, who swell the ranks of the American Civil Liberties Union and the American Jewish Congress, and often dabble in reform politics. While their rhetoric draws on the American secularist heritage, theirs is more than a simple Jeffersonian hostility to religion. These aggressive secularists do not fear religious leaders; they regard them (to the extent they think about them at all) as irrelevant fuddie-duddies (if Protestant), harmless folk humorists (if Jewish) or narrow-minded anachronisms (if Catholic). A central element of the radical secularist outlook is that public functions should be publicly performed. Nothing should be left in private hands which is arguably a matter of community concern. The pragmatic political liberalism of the 1930's and 1940's reacted against the traditional American ideology of privatism which was so often used as an excuse for not facing up to social problems. This reaction has been elevated into doctrine by the radical secularists of the 1960's. It is felt that to leave a matter to "private initiative" is to insure that it will be done incompetently, prejudicially or not at all.

These radical secularists tend to regard private charitable activity as illusory and psychologically corrupting, and the notion of religious institutions administering public funds is anathema. Religious schools are seen as especially regressive. They are to be tolerated as an option of the ignorant, not encouraged to compete with the single legitimate dispenser of social services—the secular state. All talk of accommodation in the name of pluralism is dismissed by radical secularists as 19th-century importuning, and the argument that church-related schools might become publicly subsidized middle-class havens for whites running from Negroes and other poor people clinches their case. There is, it should be noted, a direct conflict between the radical secularist demand for governmentalization of social welfare and education, and the principle of "subsidiarity" which looms large in Catholic social thought. As formulated by Pius XI, this holds that it is "unjust" and "gravely harmful to turn over to a greater society . . . functions and services which can be performed by lesser bodies. . . ." Thus families and private associations should handle all possible functions, and nothing which they are capable of doing should be displaced "upward" to government.

Unhappily, the radical secularists tend toward ideologically uncompromising political behavior. Just as they distrust the traditional American reliance on nongovernmental action, so they tend to recoil from our traditional political ethic of bargaining and compromise. Some commentators have applauded the American separation of church and state precisely because it is leavened with pragmatic exceptions (bus transportation of parochial school students) and lovable anomalies (chaplains in Congress). These, it is suggested, prove the capacity of resourceful people to come up with adjustments that work. To the radical secularist this is sentimental nonsense. The exceptions to the rule of strict separation are embarrassments to be eliminated at the first opportunity. In the battle over the Blaine Amendment in New York, radical secularists within the liberal community proved themselves as capable of fanaticism as militant Catholics and conservative Protestants.

A final indicator pointing to a future of church-state stalemate is found in recent sociological writing. Differences of (and over) religion have been politically important throughout our history.[6] There is some evidence that identification as a Protestant, Catholic or Jew is becoming more important than ethnic and regional identifications, and is assuming a place, along with socio-economic status, as one of the most significant axes of differentiation (objective and subjective) within our society. As Gerhard Lenski put it in his conclusion to *The Religious Factor:*

> The findings of this study force us to consider the possibility that American society is moving (though admittedly slowly) toward a "compartmentalized society" of the type found in contemporary Holland and Lebanon . . . In these societies most of the major institutional systems are obliged to take account of socio-religious distinctions. Hence, political parties, families, sports teams, and even business establishments are often identified with one or another of the major groups . . . The old American ideal of a great melting pot out of which would someday emerge a new, unified nation seems to have been abandoned, and we hear discussions about "pluralistic society." "Pluralistic society" may be a real alternative to "compartmentalized society," but present-day proponents of pluralism do not seem greatly concerned with making the distinction. This suggests that "pluralistic society" may turn out to be merely an-

other term, a polite euphemism, for "compartmentalized society," or
at least a steppingstone leading to it.[7]

The Detroit Area Study, of which Lenski's survey of religious attitudes and affiliations was a part, was an extensive and careful piece of
social scientific research. Though by no means universally accepted,
Lenski's findings command at least respectful hearing.

All this, then, would seem to indicate an amplification of the underlying sources of church-state conflicts: traditionally separationist Protestant denominations are growing larger; Catholic interest in public
support (at least for schools) is becoming more acute; a radical secularist ideology has taken root within some sectors of the liberal community; and religion is becoming more significant as a boundary between
social groupings.

TOWARD ECUMENICAL INDIFFERENCE

But we need not let these facts lead us to an inference of increasing
church-state stalemate. In order to judge sensibly what is happening to
the underlying sources of church-state conflict it is necessary to look at
more than the Southern Baptist growth rate and the escalating demands of church-school partisans. It will be recalled that the underlying
sources of conflict were originally characterized as ideological, psychological and structural. I am satisfied that within each of these cate-
gories the sources of tension are abating significantly.

Ideology

It is true that the Southern Baptists are growing, and it is probably
true, as Lenski suggests, that religious identifications are becoming
more important axes of social differentiation in America. But these
signs become a lot less menacing when we remind ourselves that identification with a religious subcommunity, and even church attendance,
do not necessarily mean that people are taking religious *ideology* seriously. Indeed, many of the same students who have commented on the
importance of Protestant-Catholic-Jewish identifications in the structure of contemporary society, also comment on the extent to which
these "former faiths" are becoming "culture religions" with the old
doctrines, beliefs and distinctive attitudes quietly shed. If the major
religious groupings become simply federations of fellowship-and-good-
works societies, distinguished from one another only by colorful rituals
derived from largely forgotten traditions and theologies, then there is

little to fear from church-state trigger issues. There may be some competition among the various societies and federations, but there will be few leaders interested in holy wars in defense of principles.*

Within Protestantism, this erosion of doctrine and belief seems well advanced. Lenski remarked of the Protestants in his sample that

> Many people are confused about the precise nature of Protestantism. Protestantism has become so identified with economic success, respectability, and middle-class virtues that large numbers of the clergy and laity alike appear to have lost sight of basic spiritual goals.

The old sharp conceptions of "God" and "good" are increasingly giving way to what Martin Marty has called the "God of religion-in-general." Ironically, the increase in church memberships during 1950's and early 1960's seems to have accelerated the dilution of doctrine.

> Particularity is challenged by a blurry, generalizing religion; distinctive witness is confronted by amiable syncretism; theological content is often replaced by sentiments about religion.[9]

To the extent that church-state conflicts arise out of a *doctrinal* commitment on the part of Protestants, we can look for them to decline. Even the Southern Baptist separationist ideology is showing signs of wear. Despite the continued separationist pronouncements of certain prominent Baptists, quiet change is taking place. Southern Baptist colleges are sorely tempted by the newly available federal aid, and in 1965 a commission of the Convention was appointed to "re-examine" strict separationism. Convention President Wayne Dehoney explained to the press, "We now realize that the traditional pat answer of absolute separation of church and state is no longer adequate in all situations."[10] Dehoney was vigorously criticized by co-religionists who, like E. S. James of the *Texas Baptist Standard,* continue to hold that "government aid to church institutions is fundamentally wrong." But the ultimate recommendation of the commission was that the trustees of individual Southern Baptist colleges make their own decisions on aid, and it seems that many of them shortly will be "on the take." Three years ago the South Carolina Baptist Convention forced Furman University to return a $611,898 federal construction grant, and assumed the

---

*It should not be supposed from this treatment that I regard this development as good. I do not. The point is only that it *is* happening and it *will* cool off the politics of church and state.

obligation itself. This has proved no small burden for the Convention, and it is unlikely that there will be many more such heroic gestures.

Further, it is not clear that radical secularism has the potential of becoming a major "ideologizing" force in America or even within American liberalism. Despite the vocalism of the radical secularists, the dominant style within the forces of political reform is still easy-going pragmatism. Privately, for instance, there is increasing criticism by liberal spokesmen with good credentials who argue that the American Civil Liberties Union's strict separationism is getting in the way of the support for innovation in welfare and education which should have top priority with all good liberals. Besides the radical secularists there are many (probably more) secularists who, while suspicious of churches, are willing to use them and are reluctant to let disputes over separation hold up desired programs. The American political culture is uncongenial to the ideologue and the doctrinaire, and this weighs heavily against the radical secularist. Peter Viereck once remarked that "Catholic-baiting is the anti-Semitism of the liberals," and while this is still true, it is also true that it is being driven underground. These days, even at the most liberal cocktail parties, one must take a careful look around before risking an anti-Catholic remark. John XXIII and Vatican II have had their consequences even among the unchurched intelligensia.

There are also signs that Jewish defensiveness (the basis of Jewish separationism) may be abating. In a 1966 article in *Commentary,* Milton Himmelfarb developed a powerful case for reassessing the Jewish separationist commitment. He argued that the regimes which make it toughest on Jews today are not those (such as England, Denmark and Holland) which cooperate in substantial ways with religious institutions, but rather such "enlightened" and determinedly secularist regimes as the Soviet Union. More importantly, he affirmed that adherence to an outworn and extreme separationism increasingly puts Jews in the position of opposing social welfare legislation which embodies values superior to those served by strict separation.

What if the benefits of educational programs cannot readily be extended to children outside their non-public school? What if excluding a church or a church-related institution in this or that neighborhood weakens the effort to help the poor raise themselves out of poverty? Your single-minded separationist, after first trying to deny that your questions are real questions, can say nothing. Creditably, American liberalism in general does not accept this kind of hard-heartedness. The separationists make the usual defense in such cases: it is not really we who are hard-hearted but the other fellow, to whom we refuse to pay blackmail and who has maneuvered us into a false position. They may believe this, but whenever I hear or read Jewish separationists weighing the claim of the poor against the claim of separationism, their emotion goes to separationism. Yet we are still fond of thinking of ourselves rahamanim bene rahamanim, the compassionate sons of compassionate fathers.[11]

Most important, perhaps ideological erosion is taking place in Roman Catholicism. The tripping away of encumbering received doctrine which has taken place since Vatican II is surely the most remarkable religious development of the decade, and finds a parallel only in the erosion and relativization of Marxist-Leninist revolutionary doctrine in the Soviet Union since 1955. To take one example, it was only a few years ago that astute observers were predicting a wrenching political conflict over publicly sponsored birth control programs. It was clear that government was becoming inevitably involved in furthering the use of artificial contraceptives, and it seemed that this would result in a confrontation pitting the Catholics against everyone else. Such a confrontation, it was suggested, might "re-isolate" the Catholic community, and force it once again to turn inward rather than reaching out to the larger society; such a conflict might even create the sort of deep estrangement between major sectors of the American population which has been the cause of so much instability in other political systems. But the Church's gradual dismantling of the anticontraception ideology now has reduced the possibility of such a confrontation to the vanishing point. As Peter Berger has remarked, "Now that the Catholics are changing on birth control, it is hard to say what a Catholic moral position would be."[12]

It is well to remember that while Catholic *leaders* in New York were very active in their opposition to the Blaine Amendment, the church-state issue apparently was relatively unimportant for large numbers of Catholic voters. Nassau County (on Long Island), which is approximately 50 percent Catholic, had less than 25 percent of its electorate voting for the proposed constitution which included the repeal of Blaine. Other considerations seem to have displaced church-state relations for many Catholics, and this is probably not unrelated to the general erosion of commitment to doctrine. The evidence is strong that in areas of New York where Catholic parents were using public schools, they voted their pocketbooks (or what they believed to be their pocketbooks) rather than the historic and reiterated position of their church.

Throughout American society, there is less concern with long-standing ideologies and doctrines, and more for getting things done and reducing community tensions. Few are willing to offend their neighbors (and possibly "stop progress" or "pay more") over some awkward principle. As the holding power of religious doctrine declines, and a fuzzy notion of good works takes its place, church-state tension will abate.

Psychology

Furthermore, the crumbling ideologies will probably be accompanied by an abatement of psychological tensions—of feelings of separateness and antipathy. Catholics do not seem as "foreign" as they did twenty years ago, and Protestants are less frequently pictured by Catholics as cultural imperialists. Jews enjoy a security in American life which is quite unshaken by the fitful breezes of anti-Semitism which still stir. In E. S. Bogardus' terms, there seems less perception of social distance between members of the "three great faiths."[13] Almost fifteen years ago, Gordon Allport suggested that "prejudice" broke down when individuals from socially distant aggregates (Negroes, whites, Catholics, Protestants, etc.) interacted on a basis of equality.[14] This, as was suggested in the original discussions of the psychological sources of church-state tensions, is precisely what is happening today. Hardly a day goes by without the news of some joint religious service or project involving Protestants, Catholics and Jews. The National Council of Churches is even cooperating in a joint legal action with the United States Catholic Conference in civil rights cases.

The element of "prejudice," as was previously suggested, is difficult to measure and describe with precision. Yet it is of considerable importance to an understanding of what is happening to the politics of church and state. I do not *know*, in any scientifically defensible sense, that Protestants, Catholics and Jews are coming to regard one another with less suspicion and hostility. I cannot prove this any more than I can prove that there was an amplification of Protestant-Catholic animus in the wake of World War II. The best that can be said is that this is how things appear to be going. After all, the ill feelings which grew up between Protestants and Catholics in the late 1940's and early 1950's (and gave rise to Americans United and the bruising battle over the Clark nomination) seems to have been related to changes in status.

It was an assertiveness on the part of a newly self-conscious Catholic community, and a resentment on the part of Protestants displaced from cultural pre-eminence, which heated the conflicts. Now Catholics appear less as alien interlopers, and they, in turn, feel more confident vis-a-vis Protestants. It is true that there are reminders of past inferior status (e.g., the Blaine Amendment in New York), which are resented by some. But it is at least arguable that major traumas of status re-alignment (from Protestant domination to condominium) are behind us.[15]

There is even a coming together of liturgies and what might be called "styles" of religious participation. The vernacular mass is the most dramatic sign of this homogenization, and what Americans do in their sabbath observations is certainly becoming similar to the point of experiencing the same "folk" and "rock" heresies. There are still differences in symbols which are sufficient to support feelings of distinctiveness, but it is unlikely that these will be sufficiently great to generate fear and hostility.

Structure

Finally, there are indications that the churches are becoming more similar structurally.

Vatican II dealt a death blow to the notion that all teaching in Catholic schools need be intermingled with religious instruction, and though the process is slow, the parochial schools are gradually "de-Catholicising." With the prospect of governmental aid for "secular" subjects and activities, Catholic educators are becoming increasingly "realistic" about eliminating religious symbols and practices which might be disqualifying in the eyes of supervising public authorities. We are a long way from seeing Catholic schools which are as modestly Catholic as Groton, say, is Episcopalian, but it is clear that "the parochials" are coming to look more like the American stereotype of "school" and less like something different with its own mysterious ways and appurtenances.

We have noted the increasing involvement of Jews and Protestants in private education as the middle-class demand increases. While Baptists, Methodists, Presbyterians and the Third Force sects, the most separationist of the Protestant bodies, have not yet been attracted into elementary and secondary education, yet their welfare activities are extensive, and they are increasingly tempted by government contracts for various sorts of good works—from health care to Head Start programs.

One is drawn at least to speculate as to whether the political, social and cultural forces of the latter 20th century are not forcing the institutions called churches and synagogues toward a common structural form.[16]

Structural change will probably proceed much more slowly than ideological erosion and the slackening of animosities among creeds. But the movement which can be presently observed seems clearly to be producing similarity rather than diversity. That Protestant churches are experimenting with parochial schools and Catholic churches are experimenting with Sunday schools does not mean that church-state troubles are over, but it must be set down as a positive sign.

CONCLUSION

If I am right, and the underlying sources of church-state conflict are abating, we are left with an interesting problem. The "source curve" is declining, but the "trigger-issue curve" is still rising. With government doing more and the occasions for church-state conflict arising more frequently, the question is whether the downward slope of the source curve is steep enough to forestall paralyzing conflicts in the immediate future. Ecumenical indifference is gradually relaxing the underlying sources of tension, but the potential for conflict is still substantial. The linking of church-state issues with racial issues could yet give us a great deal of trouble. Things will eventually get better, but they could first get worse. Other states may pay the price in disruption that New York has recently paid, and the politics of church and state will be a factor in social policy-making for a long time to come.

A final word. I have discussed grave issues of civic morality in an amoral fashion, and I have treated the politics of church and state in terms of its disruptive potential for the political system rather than as a confrontation of right and wrong. Instead of dealing with the strengths and weaknesses and motivations of the various actors, it may be suggested that I should have explained which side was "right." Yet this is precisely what the dialogue over church and state in America does not need. As was noted in Chapter I, accommodationist and separationist tracts abound. There are several new ones on my table as I write. If research in the social sciences teaches anything, it is that there may be questions about a political conflict just as important as who is "right" or who "ought" to win. The wider implications of church-state politics have been almost completely ignored, and it was this oversight which I set out to remedy.

NOTES

Chapter I

[1] Thomas G. Sanders, *Protestant Concepts of Church and State* (New York: Holt, Rinehart and Winston, 1964).

[2] Ernst Troeltsch, *The Social Teaching of the Christian Churches* (New York: Macmillan, 1931).

[3] See the brief but sensitive treatment of this problem by John P. Roche, "American Liberty: An Examination of the 'Tradition' of Freedom," Milton R. Konvitz and Clinton Rossiter, eds., *Aspects of Liberty* (Ithaca, New York: Cornell University Press, 1958).

[4] Winthrop S. Hudson, *American Protestantism* (Chicago: University of Chicago Press, 1961), pp. 44–45.

[5] For a somewhat different interpretation, see Benjamin A. Reist, "Church and State in America," in Robert Lee and Martin E. Marty, *Religion and Social Conflict* (New York: Oxford University Press, 1964).

[6] Quoted in Sidney E. Mead, *The Lively Experiment* (New York: Harper and Row, 1963), p. 58.

[7] On erosion see Martin E. Marty, *The New Shape of American Religion* (New York: Harpers, 1958).

[8] This general point was made elegantly by the late Mark De Wolfe Howe in his *The Garden and The Wilderness* (Chicago: University of Chicago Press, 1965).

[9] See Leonard W. Levy, *Jefferson and Civil Liberties: The Darker Side* (Cambridge: Harvard University Press, 1963), pp. 3–15; and Robert M. Healy, *Jefferson on Religion in Public Education* (New Haven: Yale University Press, 1962).

[10] Richard L. Rubenstein, "Church and State: The Jewish Posture," in Donald A. Giannella, *Religion and the Public Order, 1963* (Chicago: University of Chicago Press, 1964), p. 152.

[11] Norman St. John-Stevan, *Life, Death and the Law* (New York: Meridian Books edition, 1964), p. 31. Calvin took a different view of the state, but American Protestantism has been much more Lutheran than Calvinist in this respect. It is also interesting that European Lutheran thought ultimately came to accept the notion of establishment. In America Luther's negative view of the state was translated into separationist doctrine.

[12] John Courtney Murray, *We Hold These Truths* (Garden City, New York: Image Books edition, 1964), pp. 72–73.

13 *Ibid.*, pp. 150–53. Also see Bernard J. Coughlin's carefully argued *Church and State in Social Welfare* (New York: Columbia University Press, 1965).

14 Robert F. Drinin, *Religion, the Courts, and Public Policy* (New York: McGraw-Hill, 1963).

15 Jerome G. Kerwin, *The Catholic Viewpoint on Church and State* (Garden City, New York: Doubleday, 1960).

16 William O'Brien, *Justice Reed and the First Amendment* (Washington, D.C.: Georgetown University Press, 1948).

17 James M. O'Neill, *Catholicism and American Freedom* (New York: Harper Brothers, 1952).

18 Murray, *op. cit.*, p. 63.

19 For a case study in creedal animosity see, Kenneth Wilson Underwood, *Protestant and Catholic* (Boston: Beacon Press, 1957). For Catholic perceptions of Protestants see Robert D. Cross, *The Emergence of Liberal Catholicism in America* (Cambridge: Harvard University Press, 1958).

20 Ray Allen Billington, *The Protestant Crusade, 1800–1860* (New York: Macmillan, 1938); and John Higham, *Strangers in the Land*, rev. ed. (New York: Atheneum, 1963). See also Donald L. Kinzer, *An Episode in Anti-Catholicism: The American Protective Association* (Seattle: University of Washington Press, 1964).

21 Daniel Bell, *The Radical Right* (Garden City, New York: Anchor books, 1963). See also Richard Hofstadter, *The Paranoid Style in American Politics* (New York: Knopf, 1965).

22 Joseph R. Gusfield, *Symbolic Crusade* (Urbana: University of Illinois Press, 1963).

23 Nelson W. Polsby, "Toward an Explanation of McCarthyism," 8 *Political Studies* 224 (1962).

24 On this subject see Lawrence H. Fuchs, *John F. Kennedy and American Catholicism* (New York: Meredith, 1967).

25 *New York Times,* November 17, 1946.

26 *New York Times,* May 8, 1947.

27 *Ibid.*

28 *Ibid.*

29 *Ibid.*

30 Charles Y. Glock and Rodney Stark, *Christian Beliefs and Anti-Semitism* (New York: Harper and Row, 1966), pp. 60–80.

31 Edward Duff, "A Catholic Look at Religious Liberty," *Cross Currents,* Winter 1963, p. 56. Quoted in Earl Raab, ed., *Religious Conflict in America* (Garden City, New York: Anchor Books edition, 1964), p. 18.

32 For an analysis of church-state issues as factors in the federal policy-making process, see George R. LaNoue, *The Politics of Church and State* (New Haven: Yale University Press, forthcoming).

33 The normative implications of this problem are considered in Herbert Stroup, *Church and State in Confrontation* (N.Y.: Seabury Press, 1967), p. 180 *et passim.*

34 Two recent studies present detailed data on the Catholic school system: Andrew M. Greeley and Peter H. Rossi, *The Education of American Catholics* (Chicago: Aldine, 1966); and Reginald A. Neuwien, ed., *Catholic Schools in Action* (South Bend: University of Notre Dame Press, 1966).

35 I have no really good data on the magnitude of this "independent school explosion." As far as I know nobody has, and this is surprising since it is a

development of the greatest importance for the future of American education. Many commentators have noted it, and it is much discussed in educational circles.

[36] Murray, *op. cit.,* p. 147.

[37] *New York Times,* May 28, 1967.

[38] "Tax Exemption and the Church," *Christianity Today.* August 3, 1959, p. 7.

[39] "Tax Organized Religion," *Playboy,* April 1967, p. 114. See also Martin A. Larsen, *Church Wealth and Business Income* (New York: Philosophical Library, 1964).

[40] Dean M. Kelley, "What Part Should the Federal Government Play in Constructing Schools?" draft, typescript, 1966, p. 12.

[41] *New York Times,* October 9, 1966.

[42] *New York Times,* December 5, 1966.

[43] *New York Times,* February 6, 1967.

[44] *New York Times,* March 28, 1967.

[45] *New York Times,* April 6, 1967.

[46] "The Public Schools are Failing," *The Saturday Evening Post,* April 23, 1966; and "Is the Public School Obsolete?" 2 *Public Interest* 18 (1966).

[47] One such experimental school has already been established in Boston. *New York Times,* April 27, 1967.

[48] Harvey Pressman, *New Schools for the Poor: Designs for Equality and Excellence,* Lincoln Filene Center for Citizenship and Public Affairs, 1966, mimeo, p. iii.

[49] See Virgil C. Blum, "This Heartless Business," *America,* September 10, 1966.

Chapter II

[1] Peter H. Odegard, *Pressure Politics: The History of the Anti-Saloon League* (New York: Columbia University Press, 1928).

[2] *New York Times,* January 30, 1964.

[3] Murray S. Stedman, Jr., *Religion and Politics in America* (New York: Harcourt, Brace and World, 1964), pp. 94–95.

[4] From *Wake Up America!* an undated Americans United pamphlet.

[5] Theodore C. Sorenson, *Kennedy* (New York: Harper's, 1964), p. 144.

[6] 374 U.S. 398 (1963).

[7] Will Maslow, "The Legal Defense of Religious Liberty—The Strategy and Tactics of the American Jewish Congress," paper delivered before the 1961 annual meeting of the American Political Science Association, p. 15.

[8] Sterling M. McMurrin, "The U.S. Office of Education: An Inside View," *Saturday Review,* February 16, 1963, p. 78.

[9] Ralph Lord Roy, *Apostles of Discord* (Boston: Beacon, 1953), pp. 147 *et passim.*

[10] For the best treatment of interest groups in New York City politics, see Wallace S. Sayre and Herbert Kaufman, *Governing New York City* (New York: Norton paperback edition, 1964), pp. 42 *et passim.*

[11] Unhappily, there is no scholarly analysis of the political behavior of the Catholic hierarchy. While he would certainly not have subscribed to the terms I have employed, a useful short history is John Tracy Ellis, *American Catholicism* (Chicago: University of Chicago Press, 1956).

[12] These briefs are reproduced in full in 50 *Georgetown Law Journal* 397 (1961).

[13] John C. Bennett, *Christians and the State* (New York: Scribner's, 1958),

[14] 268 U.S. 510 (1925).

Chapter III

[1] The works of Leo Pfeffer are an excellent example of such purposeful history from a separationist viewpoint. See especially his *Church, State and Freedom* (rev. ed.; Boston: Beacon, 1966). On the accommodationist side, two recent contributions are: Charles E. Rice, *The Supreme Court and Public Prayer* (New York: Fordham University Press, 1964); and Joseph E. Constanza, *This Nation under God* (New York: Herder and Herder, 1964).

[2] Quoted in Leonard W. Levy, *Jefferson and Civil Liberties: The Darker Side* (Cambridge: Harvard University Press, 1963), p. 12.

[3] 330 U.S. 1 (1947).

[4] 330 U.S. at 15–16.

[5] 330 U.S. at 24.

[6] 330 U.S. at 58–59.

[7] See *McCollum v. Board of Education*, 333 U.S. 203 (1948); and *Zorach v. Clauson*, 343 U.S. 306 (1952).

[8] See *Engle v. Vitale*, 370 U.S. 421 (1962); *Murray v. Curlett*, 374 U.S. 203 1963); and *Abington School District v. Schempp*, 374 U.S. 203 (1963).

[9] See George R. La Noue, "The Child Benefit Theory Revisited," 13 *Journal of Public Law* 76 (1964).

[10] La Noue is presently completing extensive work on the administration of the ESEA in New Jersey which, he argues, justifies his pessimism.

[11] *New York Times,* June 27, 1962.

[12] *Ibid.*

[13] *Ibid.*

[14] *New York Times,* June 18, 1963.

[15] *Ibid.*

[16] The best item in a growing literature on interest-group lobbying in the constitutional arena is Clement E. Vose, *Caucasians Only* (Berkeley: University of California Press, 1959).

[17] *Griffen v. School Board,* 377 U.S. 218 (1964).

[18] Maslow, *loc. cit.*

[19] 262 U.S. 447.

[20] *Ibid.*, at 488–89.

[21] On this subject, see Louis L. Jaffe, "Standing to Secure Judicial Review: Public Actions," 74 *Harvard Law Review* 1265 (1961); Note, "Taxpayer Suits: A Survey and Summary," 69 *Yale Law Journal* (1960); and the Arthur Garfield Hays Civil Liberties Conference, "Public Aid to Parochial Schools and Standing to Bring Suit," 12 *Buffalo Law Review* 34 (1962).

[22] Senate Report No. 1403, 89th Congress, 2nd Session, p. 4.

[23] *Judicial Review,* Hearings before the Subcommittee on Constitutional Rights of the Senate Committee on the Judiciary, 89th Congress, 2nd session, Parts I and II.

[24] Some of the best recent writing on lobbying in Congress and the executive branch is found in Douglass Cater, *Power in Washington* (New York: Knopf, 1961); Lester Milbrath, *The Washington Lobbyists* (Chicago: Rand-McNally, 1963); Richard F. Fenno, Jr., *The Power of the Purse* (Boston: Little, Brown, 1966), and Andrew W. Scott and Margaret A. Hunt, *Congress and Lobbies* (Chapel Hill: University of North Carolina Press, 1965).

[25] Hugh Douglas Price, "Race, Religion, and the Rules Committee," Alan F. Westin, ed., *The Uses of Power* (New York: Harcourt, Brace and World, 1961), p. 70.

[26] This meeting is one of those things about which people are willing to talk but not be quoted.

[27] This account relies heavily on Dean M. Kelley and George R. La Noue, "The Church-State Settlement in the Federal Aid to Education Act: A Legislative History," in Donald A. Gianella, *Religion and the Public Order*, 1965 (Chicago: University of Chicago Press, 1966). Both the authors were intimately involved in the politics they describe. There is unfortunately, no treatment of these events from an accommodationist viewpoint.

[28] Public Law No. 10, 89th Congress, 1st session, (April 11, 1965).

[29] Congressional Record 5572 (1965).

[30] *Ibid.* at 5792.

[31] Kelley and La Noue, *op. cit.*, pp. 159–61.

[32] House Report No. 1814, 89th Congress, 2nd session, (1966), p. 4.

[33] House Report No. 1814; Part 2, 89th Congress, 2nd session, (1966).

[34] *New York Times*, April 5, 1967.

[35] *New York Times*, April 25, 1955.

[36] Quoted in *New York Times*, April 18, 1955.

[37] *Ibid.*

[38] *New York Times*, November 27, 1957.

Chapter IV

[1] This is not to suggest that there was anything dishonest about the scholar incentive program. It may be unconstitutional, but it is not mean or disreputable.

[2] See the *New York Times*, March 2, April 28, May 8, May 17 and May 19, 1966.

[3] *New York Times*, May 21, 1966.

[4] Interview with Mr. Aryeh Neier, February 9, 1968.

[5] *New York Times*, August 20, 1966.

[6] *Ibid.*

[7] *Ibid.*

[8] *New York Times*, September 15, 1966.

[9] *New York Times*, October 25, 1966.

[10] *New York Times*, January 1, 1967.

[11] 20 New York 2d 109 (1967).

[12] *New York Times*, March 5, 1967.

[13] The Very Reverend Eugene J. Malloy, "Statement Before the New York City Board of Education," August 17, 1966, p. 1.

[14] *New York Times*, August 8, 1966.

[15] Molloy, *op. cit.*, p. 2.

[16] *New York Times*, November 9, 1967.

[17] The Very Reverend Eugene J. Molloy, "Statement Before the New York City Board of Education," November 14, 1966, p. 1.

[18] *New York Times*, November 18, 1966.

[19] *Flast v. Gardner*, 271 F. Supp. 1 (1967).

[20] For professional litigants winning at the lower court level is sometimes a mixed blessing. An example of such a frustrating victory is *Swart v. South Burlington*. The case was brought by Americans United challenging the practice of certain Vermont townships which, having no public high school, paid tuition for their young people at neighboring public *and parochial* institutions. The Vermont Supreme Court disallowed the tuition to church-related schools on federal constitutional grounds, and a U.S. Supreme Court test was never achieved.

[21] *New York Times,* October 18, 1966.

[22] *New York Times,* August 23, 1967.

[23] *New York Times,* August 15, 1966.

[24] *Civil Liberties in New York,* October, 1966, p. 2.

[25] *The Transcript of Public Hearings,* Temporary Commission, December, 1966, fairly bristles with charges of racial and religious prejudice.

[26] An excellent account of the politics of the 1894 convention is found in John Webb Pratt, *Religion, Politics and Diversity* (Ithaca: Cornell University Press, 1967), pp. 225–56.

[27] *New York Times,* October 5, 1966.

[28] See Harry W. Jones, "State Aid and Church-Related Schools," 28 *Proceedings of the Academy of Political Science* 347–48 (1967).

[29] *New York Times,* October 6, 1966.

[30] *New York Times,* October 12 and 22, 1966.

[31] *New York Times,* October 18, 1966.

[32] *New York Times,* October 19, 1966.

[33] *New York Times,* October 22, 1966.

[34] *New York Times,* October 23, 1966.

[35] Interview with Mr. Lester Greenberg, an official of PEARL and the AJCongress, February 23, 1968.

[36] *New York Times,* March 26, 1967.

[37] "Constitutional Confrontation in New York State," *Christian Century,* July 19, 1966.

[38] Minutes of these meetings are in the files of the Commission on Law and Social Action of the AJCongress. Topics discussed included upstate organization and involving Negro groups in the battle to retain Blaine.

[39] Interview with Mr. Lester Greenberg, February 23, 1968.

[40] *New York Times,* April 30, 1967.

[41] *New York Times,* March 31, 1967.

[42] *New York Times,* March 29, 1967.

[43] *New York Times,* July 13, 1967.

[44] *Transcript of Public Hearings,* Temporary Commission, December 1966, p. 5 ff.

[45] *New York Times,* July 23, 1967.

[46] *New York Times,* July 8, 1967.

[47] *New York Times,* July 20, 1967.

[48] Andrew Hacker, "The Blaine Amendment—Yes or No?" *New York Times Magazine,* October 1, 1967.

[49] *New York Times,* August 16, 1967.

[50] *New York Times,* August 17, 1967.

[51] This is based on my conversations in Albany with delegates and staff members who not only wished to go unquoted, but to forget the whole thing.

[52] *New York Times,* October 31, 1967.

[53] *New York Times,* October 21, 1967.

[54] *New York Times,* November 10, 11, 12 and 14.

[55] *New York Times,* September 31, 1967.

[56] *New York Times,* September 3, 1967.

Chapter V

[1] James S. Coleman, "Social Cleavage and Religious Conflict," in Raab, *op. cit.,* p. 92.

[2] Peter F. Drucker, "On the 'Economic Basis' of American Politics," 10 *Public Interest* at 35 (1968).

[3] This is certainly true of such past presidents as Herschel Hobbs, and publicists such as E. S. James, of the *Texas Baptist Standard*.

[4] Statistics on religion in America are notoriously spotty and unreliable (separationist groups have blocked the inclusion of a "religion" question in the decennial census), and comparative growth rates are particularly so. The most trustworthy source is the Yearbook of American Churches, published by the NCC, and edited, until his death in 1966, by Benson Y. Landis.

[5] *New York Times,* August 20, 1967.

[6] See, for instance, Seymour Martin Lipset, "Religion and Politics in American History," in Raab, *op. cit.*

[7] Gerhard, Lenski, *The Religious Factor* (Garden City: Anchor Books edition, 1963), pp. 363–364.

[8] *Ibid.,* p. 352.

[9] Marty, *op. cit.,* p. 2.

[10] *New York Times,* November 28, 1965.

[11] Milton Himmelfarb, "Church and State: How High a Wall?", *Commentary,* July, 1966, p. 25.

[12] Quoted in New York Times, February 25, 1968. See also Dr. Berger's *The Noise of Solemn Assemblies* (Garden City: Doubleday, 1961).

[13] For an interesting application of Bogardus' concept of social distance see Gordon W. Allport, *The Nature of Prejudice* (Garden City: Anchor Books edition, 1958), pp. 35–38.

[14] *Ibid.,* pp. 250–267.

[15] An excellent article of this point is Will Herberg, "Religious Group Conflict," in Lee and Marty, *op. cit.*

[16] In this connection it is interesting to consider the predictions concerning religion in America generated by the Commission on the Year 2000 of the American Academy of Arts and Sciences. See especially Krister Stendahl, "Religion, Mysticism, and the Institutional Church," 96 *Daedalus* 854 (1967).

BIBLIOGRAPHY

To attempt a comprehensive list of the works on religion and politics, or even on church and state in America, would exceed the space limitation under which this volume was undertaken. Moreover, much of the church-state literature is pure polemic and many items, addressed to the conditions and issues of fifteen or twenty years ago, are of interest only to professional historians.

Listed here are works which seem to me most helpful in coming to an understanding of the politics of church and state in America today.

RELIGION AND POLITICS

Books

Berger, Peter L. *The Noise of Solemn Assemblies*. Garden City, N.Y.: Doubleday, 1961.

Billington, Ray Allen. *The Protestant Crusade, 1800–1860*. New York: Macmillan, 1938.

Cogley, John (ed.). *Religion in America*. New York: Meridian Books, 1958.

Cross, Robert D. *The Emergence of Liberal Catholicism in America*. Cambridge, Mass.: Harvard University Press, 1958.

Ellis, John Tracy. *American Catholicism*. Chicago: University of Chicago Press, 1956.

Fuchs, Lawrence H. *John F. Kennedy and American Catholicism*. New York: Meredith Press, 1967.

Glock, Charles Y. and Stark, Rodney. *Christian Beliefs and Anti-Semitism*. New York: Harper & Row, 1966.

Gusfield, Joseph R. *Symbolic Crusade*. Urbana: University of Illinois Press, 1963.

147

Higham, John. *Strangers in the Land.* Rev. ed. New York: Atheneum, 1963.

Hofstadter, Richard. *The Paranoid Style in American Politics.* New York: Knopf, 1965.

Hudson, Winthrop S. *American Protestantism.* Chicago: University of Chicago Press, 1959.

Kinzer, Donald L. *An Episode in Anti-Catholicism: The American Protective Association.* Seattle: University of Washington Press, 1964.

LaNoue, George R. (ed.). *A Bibliography of Doctoral Dissertations on Politics and Religion.* New York: National Council of Churches, 1963.

Lenski, Gerhard. *The Religious Factor.* Rev. ed. Garden City, N. Y.: Doubleday, 1963.

Marty, Martin E. *The New Shape of American Religion.* New York: Harper & Brothers, 1958.

Mead, Sidney E. *The Lively Experiment.* New York: Harper & Row, 1963.

Nottingham, Elizabeth K. *Religion and Society.* New York: Random House, 1954.

Raab, Earl (ed.). *Religious Conflict in America.* Garden City, N. Y.: Doubleday, 1964.

Roy, Ralph Lord. *Apostles of Discord.* Boston: The Beacon Press, 1953.

Stark, Rodney and Glock, Charles Y. *American Piety.* New York: Harper & Row, 1968.

Stedman, Murray S. *Religion and Politics in America.* New York: Harcourt, Brace & World, 1964.

Underwood, Kenneth W. *Protestant and Catholic.* Boston: The Beacon Press, 1957.

Winter, Gibson. *The Suburban Captivity of the Churches.* New York: Macmillan, 1962.

Articles

Darrow, R. Morton. "The Church and Techniques of Political Action," in Smith and Jamison (eds.), *Religious Perspectives in American Culture.* Princeton, N.J.: Princeton University Press, 1961.

Ebersole, Luke. "Religion and Politics," *The Annals,* Vol. 332 (November, 1960). (Religion in American Society)

Glock, Charles and Ringer, B. B. "Church Policy and the Attitudes of Ministers and Parishioners on Social Issues," 21 *Am. Soc. Rev.* 148 (1956).

Stark, Rodney, "Through a Stained Glass Darkly: Reciprocal Protestant-Catholic Images in America," 25 *Sociological Analysis* 159 (1964).

Symposium. "The Roman Catholic Church in America," *The Atlantic Monthly,* Vol. 210, No. 2 (August, 1962).

———. "Religion in America," *Daedalus,* Vol. 96, No. 1 (Winter, 1967).

CHURCH AND STATE

Books

Beth, Loren P. *The American Theory of Church and State.* Gainsville: University of Florida Press, 1958.

Blum, Virgil C. *Freedom in Education.* Garden City, N.Y.: Doubleday, 1965.

Coughlin, Bernard J. *Church and State in Social Welfare.* New York: Columbia University Press, 1965.

Drinan, Robert F., S.J. *Religion, the Courts, and Public Policy.* New York: McGraw-Hill, 1963.

Greene, Evarts B. *Religion and the State.* Ithaca, N.Y.: Great Seal Books, 1959.

BIBLIOGRAPHY 149

Howe, Mark DeWolfe. *The Garden and the Wilderness*. Chicago: University of Chicago Press, 1965.
Huegli, Albert G. (ed.). *Church and State Under God*. Saint Louis: Concordia Publishing House, 1964.
Katz, Wilber G. *Religion and the American Constitutions*. Evanston: Northwestern University Press, 1964.
Kauper, Paul G. *Religion and the Constitution:* Baton Rouge: Louisiana State University Press, 1964.
Kurland, Philip B. *Religion and the Law*. Chicago: Aldine, 1962.
LaNoue, George R. *The Politics of Church and State*. New Haven: Yale University Press, forthcoming.
Littell, Franklin Hamlin. *From State Church to Pluralism: A Protestant Interpretation of Religion in America*. Garden City, N.Y.: Doubleday, 1962.
Meranto, Philip. *The Politics of Federal Aid to Education in 1964: A Study in Political Innovation*. Syracuse, N.Y.: Syracuse University Press, 1967.
Murray, A. Victor. *The State and the Church in a Free Society*. Cambridge, Mass.: The Cambridge University Press, 1958.
Murray, John Courtney. *We Hold These Truths*. Garden City, N.Y.: Image Books, Doubleday, 1964.
Oaks, Dallin H. (ed.). *The Wall Between Church and State*. Chicago, Ill.: University of Chicago Press, 1963.
Pfeffer, Leo. *Church, State, and Freedom*. Rev. ed. Boston, Mass.: The Beacon Press, 1966.
Powell, Theodore. *The School Bus Law*. Middletown, Conn.: Wesleyan University Press, 1960.
Pratt, John Webb. *Religion, Politics and Diversity: The Church-State Theme in New York History*. Ithaca, N.Y.: Cornell University Press, 1967.
Regan, Richard J., S.J. *American Pluralism and the Catholic Conscience*. New York: Macmillan, 1963.
St. John-Stevas, Norman. *Life, Death and the Law*. Bloomington: Indiana University Press, 1961.
Sanders, Thomas G. *Protestant Concepts of Church and State*. New York: Holt, Rinehart & Winston, 1964.
Stokes, Anson Phelps and Pfeffer, Leo. *Church and State in the United States*. Rev. one-vol. ed. New York: Harper & Row, 1964.
Stroup, Herbert. *Church and State in Confrontation*. New York: The Seabury Press, 1967.

Articles
Block, Charles. "Religion, 'Standing,' and the Supreme Court's Role," 13 *Journal of Public Law* 459 (1964).
Choper, Jesse. "The Establishment Clause and Aid to Parochial Schools," 56 *California Law Review* 260 (1968).
Galanter, Marc. "Religious Freedoms in the United States," 1966 *Wisconsin Law Review* 217 (1966).
Gianella, Donald A. "Religious Liberty, Nonestablishment, and Doctrinal Development," Part I, 80 *Harvard Law Review* 1831 (1967), and Part II, 81 *Harvard Law Review* 513 (1968).
LaNoue, George R. "The Child Benefit Theory Revisited: Textbook, Transportation and Medical Care," 13 *Journal of Public Law* 76 (1964).
McKean, Dayton. "The State, the Church, and the Lobby," in Smith and Jamison (eds.), *Religious Perspectives in American Culture*, Vol. II. Princeton, N.J.: Princeton University Press, 1961.

Schwarz, Alan. "No Imposition of Religion: The Establishment Clause Value," 77 *Yale Law Journal* 692 (1968).

Sutherland, Arthur. "Establishment According to Engle," 76 *Harvard Law Review* 570 (1962).

Van Alstyne, Arvo. "Tax Exemption of Church Property," 20 *Ohio State Law Journal* 461 (1959).

Van Alstyne, William W. "Constitutional Separation of Church and State: The Quest for a Coherent Position," 57 *Am. P.S.R.* 865 (1963).

INTEREST GROUPS

Books

Liederman, Elias. *Unions Before the Bar.* New York: Harper Brothers, 1950.

Manwaring, David R. *Render Unto Caesar: The Flag Salute Controversy.* Chicago, Ill.: University of Chicago Press, 1962.

Olson, Mancur Jr. *The Logic of Collective Action.* Cambridge, Mass.: Harvard University Press, 1965.

Pratt, Henry Johnson. "The Protestant Council of the City of New York as a Political Interest Group." (Unpublished doctoral dissertation, Columbia University, 1962).

Truman, David B. *The Governmental Process.* New York: Knopf, 1951.

Vose, Clement E. *Caucasians Only: The Supreme Court, the NAACP, and the Restrictive Covenant Costs.* Berkeley: University of California Press, 1959.

Wolfskill, George. *The Revolt of the Conservatives: A History of the American Liberty League, 1934–1940.* Boston: Houghton Mifflin, 1962.

Zeigler, Harmon. *Interest Groups in American Society.* Englewood, N.J.: Prentice-Hall, 1964.

Articles

Birkby, Robert H. and Murphy, Walter F. "Interest Group Conflict in the Judicial Arena: The First Amendment and Group Access to the Courts," 42 *Texas Law Review* 1018 (1964).

Greenberg, Jack. "Race Relations and Group Interest in the Law," 13 *Rutgers Law Review* 503 (1959).

Jaffe, Louis: "Standing to Secure Judicial Review: Public Actions," 74 *Harvard Law Review* 1265 (1961).

Krislov, Samuel. "The Amicus Curiae Brief: From Friendship to Advocacy," 62 *Yale Law Journal* 694 (1963).

Latham, Earl. "The Group Basis of Politics: Notes for a Theory," 46 *American Political Science Review* 376 (1952).

Maslow, Will. "The Legal Defense of Religious Liberty—The Strategy and Tactics of the American Jewish Congress." Paper delivered at the 1961 Annual Meeting of the American Political Science Association.

Note, "The South's Amended Barratry Laws: An Attempt to End Group Pressure Through the Courts," 72 *Yale Law Journal* 1613 (1963).

———. "Taxpayers Suits: A Survey and Summary," 69 *Yale Law Journal* 895 (1960).

Vose, Clement E. "Interest Groups, Judicial Review, and Local Government," *The Western Political Quarterly,* Vol. XIX, No. 1 (March, 1966).

———. "Litigation as a Form of Pressure Group Activity," 319 *The Annals* 20 (1958).

———. "NAACP Strategy in the Covenant Cases," 6 *Western Reserve Law Review* 101 (1955).

———. "The National Consumers' League and the Brandeis Brief," 1 *Midwest Journal of Political Science* 267 (1957).

INDEX